OXFORD SCIENCE programme 2 E-H

Consultant Editor: **Paul Denley**

Managing Editor: **Stephen Pople**

Steering Committee:

Terry Hudson
Phil Lidstone
David Lossl
Jim Sage
Linda Scott
Stephen Stretch
Susan Williams

Oxford University Press

Contents

Module F
The active Earth

Key	
YI	Your ideas
LF	Looking further
UNI	Using new ideas

Module G
The Earth in space

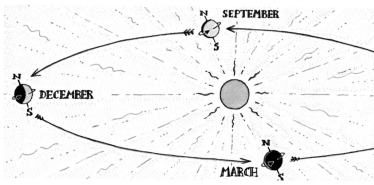

Module H
The Earth in balance

Key

YI Your ideas

LF Looking further

UNI Using new ideas

Introduction

This book is just one part of the Oxford Science Programme. Its investigations and activities have been specially designed for Key Stage 3 of the National Curriculum for Science. The book is divided into four modules, each dealing with a different aspect of science:

Module E
Sight and sound

Light is a member of a whole family of waves called the electromagnetic spectrum. Sound also travels as waves, but it does not belong to the same family as light. In this module, you look at the causes and effects of sound, the way sounds are transmitted through different materials, and how different sounds are produced by musical instruments. You investigate light, other electromagnetic waves, devices such as mirrors and cameras which use light, and human vision.

Module F
The active Earth

Our weather comes from changing conditions in the Earth's atmosphere. Over a long period of time it can alter landscapes, though flowing water has a major part to play as well. In this module, you look at the weather, how to record it and the factors which influence it. Next you consider the physical and chemical effects of weather and water, and how materials worn away from old rocks can eventually form part of new ones. Finally, you take a closer look at the origins and properties of rocks and minerals.

Module G
The Earth in space

The Earth is just one of a whole family of planets which orbits the Sun. In this module, you investigate how the motion of the Earth gives us day, night and seasons, and how conditions are different on the Moon and on other planets. You look at gravity and its effects, the problems of space travel, and people's changing ideas about the Earth over the centuries. Finally, you consider how, through plants, the Sun is the prime source of energy for all living things on Earth.

Module H
The Earth in balance

We share the Earth with many other living things and depend on them for our survival. In this module, you start by looking at some different world environments and how human activity can change and damage them. You investigate the problems of rubbish and waste disposal, and the need to recycle valuable resources. You look into fossil fuels and how their use is disturbing the balance of the atmosphere. Finally, you consider some of the causes and effects of pollution.

Each module is made up of double-page spreads, but these have been grouped in a special way. We've called each group of spreads a unit. At the start of each unit, you will be asked to think about *your* ideas and to share and discuss them with others. Next, you will carry out some investigations to test your ideas. Finally, you will have the chance to use any new ideas you have learned. So, as you work through the spreads in each unit, the pattern will be:

> your ideas
> looking further
> using new ideas

The last spread in each module is called *Stepping stones*. It will present you with new challenges covering the whole module.

Start investigating and see what you can find out!

E Sight and sound

E1.1 Noise annoyance

Stansgate Airport was built several years ago. Today, more and more passengers want to fly from the airport. But there are problems. Customer facilities need improving. The runway needs extending to take bigger jets. And the airport management would like to run night flights. At present, only daytime flights are allowed.

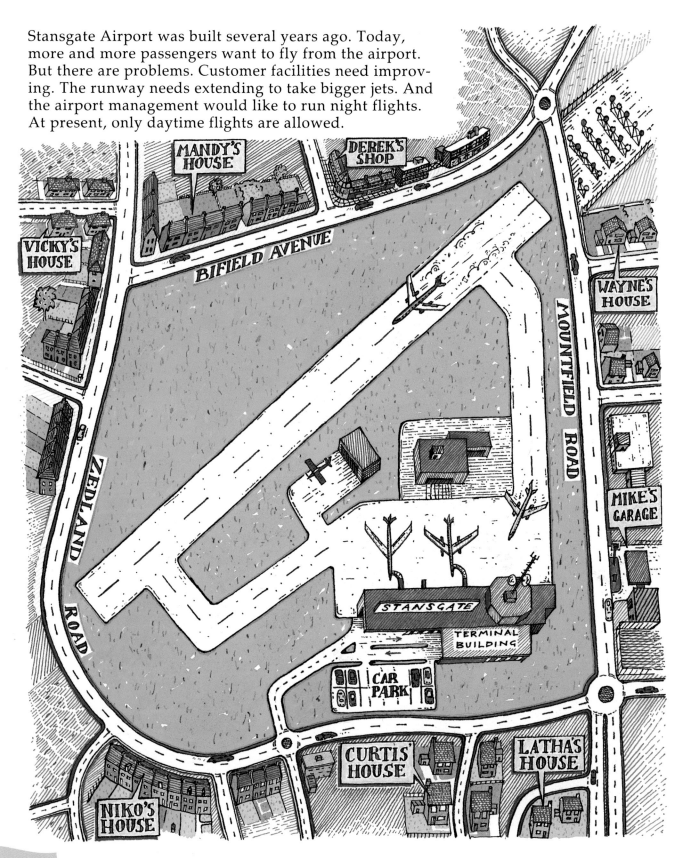

Above, are comments from people who live and work in the Stansgate area. Look at the comments, and the map on the opposite page. Then answer these questions with your group:

1. List some reasons why people might welcome an extension to the airport.
2. List some reasons why people might object to an airport extension.
3. List the different sources of noise in and around an airport.
4. Why do you think houses have not been built all the way along Zedland Road?
5. Which would be the noisier place to live, Wayne's house or Latha's house? Give a reason for your answer.
6. What did Derek mean when he said his house had been 'insulated against sound'? Give some ways in which he might have insulated his house against sound.
7. What materials do you think sound can travel through? (Remember: a material can be solid, liquid or gas.)
8. Music and noise are both sounds. So what is different about them? Make a list of your ideas.
9. What evidence is there that sound can travel in all directions?
10. What evidence is there that sound takes time to travel?

E1.2 Sounds far and near

Big caves like the ones at Cheddar and Wookey Hole get thousands of visitors every year. Some of their underground chambers are over 20 metres high. If you stand in the middle of a big cave and shout, you may hear a voice shouting back at you a fraction of a second later.

1 What is this effect called?
2 Why is there a time delay before you hear the voice?
3 In what other places might you hear the effect?
4 Why wouldn't you hear the effect if you shouted in the middle of a large, open field?

Sounds at sea

Captain Windlass was getting worried. The fog was closing in. He decided to send out regular toots on his foghorn in case there were other ships around. Every time he gave a toot, he heard an answering toot a little later. But as he steamed through the fog, the time before each answering toot got less and less! Suddenly the fog cleared. The Captain looked around but there was no other boat to be seen.

You can see Captain Windlass on his ship in the pictures.

5 Why did Captain Windlass hear a second toot after he had sounded his fog horn?
6 Make a simple sketch of the last picture and draw in the route that the sound must have taken from the foghorn.
7 Why did the time between the Captain's toot and the answering toot get less and less?
8 If you could hire the Captain's boat for the day how could you use it to measure the speed of sound?

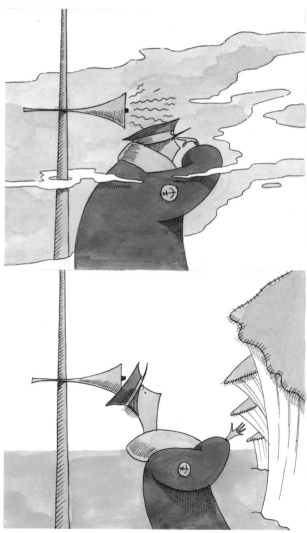

Did you know?

The speed of sound in air is about 330 metres per second (760 mph).

9 How far would sound travel in 2 seconds?

10

Making sounds

You can try making sounds using the things in the pictures.

Investigate

- Find out how many different sounds each thing can make.
- Describe how you made each sound.

Making music

With a ruler and an elastic band, you can make your own musical instruments!

Investigate

Find out how to make different notes using a ruler and an elastic band.

You need
Ruler, elastic band, pencil.

Useful information
Sounds from musical instruments are called notes. People say that high notes have a **high pitch** and that low notes have a **low pitch**.

What to do
- Hold the ruler with part of it sticking out over the edge of the bench.
  Make the ruler vibrate.
- Find out how to make the ruler produce a louder note.
- Find out how to make the ruler produce a higher note.
- Make an elastic band guitar like the one in the picture. Find out how to make it produce louder and then higher notes.
- How are the vibrations of the elastic band different if the note is louder? How are they different if the note is higher?
- Play a simple tune on each instrument.
- Find a way of writing down your tune so that another group can play it by following your instructions.

Did you know?

All sounds are caused by something vibrating. Hard, solid things vibrate when you bang them together, but the vibrations are often too small to see.

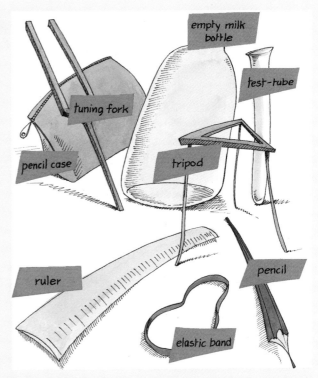

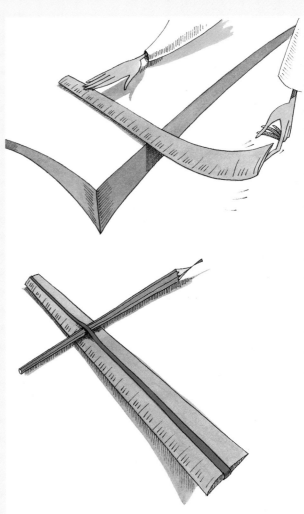

E1.3 The sounds of music

All sounds are caused by something vibrating. Sometimes you can see the vibrations. Sometimes they are too small to see. The vibrations send a series of 'squashes' through the air. These are called sound waves. They travel outwards rather like ripples rushing across the surface of a pond. When sound waves go into your ears, they set up vibrations which you hear as sound.

Looking into loudspeakers

A loudspeaker has a paper or plastic cone in it. When electrical signals are fed to the loudspeaker, the cone vibrates backwards and forwards. This sends 'squashes' out through the air.

Investigate

Use a signal generator to alter the vibrations of a loudspeaker cone. Find out how this affects the sound you hear.

You need
Loudspeaker connected to signal generator.

Useful information
- A signal generator has a dial or a display to tell you the **frequency** of the vibrations. Frequency is measured in **hertz** (**Hz** for short). If the frequency is 200 Hz the loudspeaker cone is vibrating 200 times every second and giving out 200 sound waves every second.
- A signal generator has one knob to change the frequency and another to change the loudness.

What to do
- Start with a low frequency.
  Make the sound louder.
  What happens to the vibrations of the cone?
- Slowly increase the frequency.
  What happens to the pitch of the sound?
  What happens to the vibrations of the cone?

Looking into musical instruments

Musical instruments make sounds because something vibrates inside them. It may be a vibrating string. It may be a tubeful of vibrating air. There has to be something to set off the vibrations. It could be your fingers plucking a string. It could be a tiny reed which vibrates when you blow through it. It could be a wobbling flow of air when you blow across a wedge.

Investigate

- Look at as many musical instruments as you can.
- Find out what is vibrating inside each one.
- Find out what sets off the vibrations.
- Find out how notes are made higher or lower.

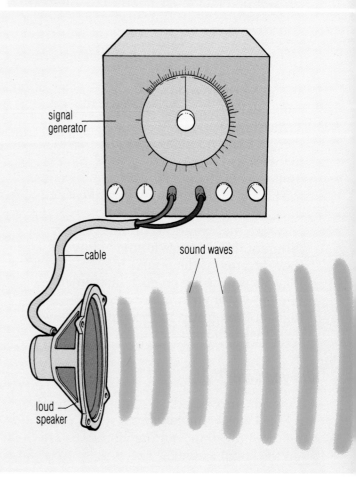

signal generator

cable

sound waves

loud speaker

- Find out how notes are made louder or quieter.
- Make a poster to show what you have found.

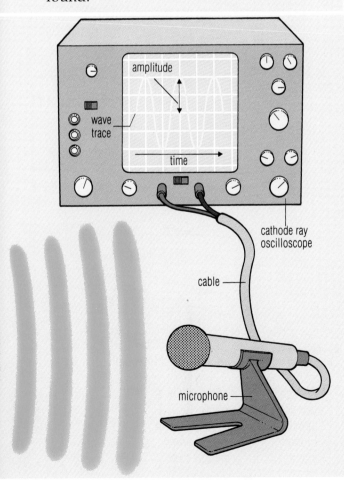

amplitude

wave trace

time

cathode ray oscilloscope

cable

microphone

Did you know?

Your voice is a kind of musical instrument with vibrating air inside. You can feel the vibrations using a blown-up balloon. Rest your fingers lightly against one side of the balloon. Then speak or hum with your mouth very close to the other side.

Looking at wave traces

You can't see sound waves. But a microphone can pick them up and use them to make electrical signals. And a cathode ray oscilloscope (CRO) can use these signals to draw a wave-like graph on its screen. This graph is called a **wave trace.**

Investigate

Use a microphone to pick up the sounds from a loudspeaker. Find out how the wave trace on an oscilloscope changes when you change the sound.

You need
Loudspeaker connected to signal generator, oscilloscope connected to microphone and adjusted by your teacher, musical instruments.

Useful information
- The wave trace is a graph showing you how the 'squashes' are arriving at the microphone.
- Distances across the screen stand for time. So a short distance from one peak to the next means a short time between one 'squash' and the next.
- The height of each peak on the wave trace is called the **amplitude**.

What to do
- Look at the wave trace when the loudspeaker is giving a continuous sound.
- What happens to the wave trace if you increase the frequency?
- What happens to the wave trace if you increase the loudness of the sound?
- Try playing the same note on different musical instruments. Draw the wave traces and compare them. What similarities can you see? What differences can you see?

E1.4 From place to place

Sounds often travel through different materials to places where people don't want to hear them. For example, the sound from a motorcycle can travel through air and glass and be heard by a person in a telephone box.

1 Study the picture. Look for situations where sounds might travel to places where they are not wanted. Show your ideas in a table like the one on the right.

Sound from....	materials	to....
motorcycle	air glass	person in telephone box

Sending sound

If materials let sound through, scientists say that they can **transmit** sound. Try testing different objects to find out which ones can transmit sound.

Investigate

- Place a piece of card over your ear. Put one end of a ruler against the card. Gently rub the other end of the ruler. Does the sound travel along the ruler?
- Now test objects like the ones listed on the right. Which ones will sound pass through?
- Make a list of those materials you have tested which can transmit sound.

Testing to see if a ruler can transmit sound.

You can try testing these objects as well:

test-tube	book
pencil	block of wood
rubber	clamp stand
stone	pencil case

Sound model

Scientists have a theory about the way sound travels. They think that air and other materials are made up of billions of tiny particles called **molecules**. These can push on each other. If, say, a loudspeaker cone is vibrating in air, its movements are passed on to the nearest particles. These push the next particles, and so on.

Investigate

Make a model to show how a movement may be passed along a line of particles.

You need
Card, five marbles

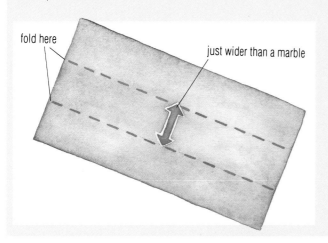

What to do

- Fold some card to make a channel for the marbles to roll along. You can see what to make in the picture.
- Rest the channel on a level bench. Put the marbles in the channel so that they are evenly spaced out.
- Imagine that the marbles are air particles and that a loudspeaker has just made the end particle move. Make the first marble move by flicking it along the channel with your finger.
- Describe what happens after you have flicked the first marble.
- Explain why you think sound takes time to travel from one place to another instead of arriving instantly.

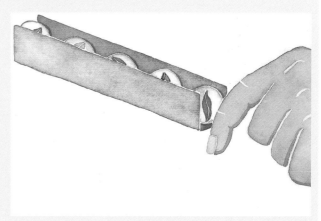

Moon talk

Nina and Glenn are walking on the Moon. They have to wear spacesuits because there is no air there. Glenn needs instructions. He asks Nina for help but his radio isn't working. Nina cannot hear him no matter how hard he shouts.

Nina touches her space helmet against Glenn's. Glenn is delighted. Now he can hear Nina's voice.

Answer these questions:

2 Why couldn't Nina hear Glenn, even though he was shouting.

3 When the helmets touched, what did Nina's voice have to travel through to reach Glenn?

4 Scientists think that radio waves are very different from sound waves. What evidence could Nina and Glenn give for this?

E1.5 Sound insulation

Remember the noise problems at Stansgate Airport? Here are some investigations that might help solve some of them.

Stopping the rattles

Jo the catering manager complains that the tables in the restaurant vibrate and rattle whenever an aircraft takes off. The tables are fixed to the floor. Jo wonders if the vibrations could be reduced by fixing some material between the table legs and the floor.

Investigate

Test some materials to find out which ones are best at reducing vibrations.

You need
Ruler, materials to test, items chosen by you.

Useful information
The picture shows one way of testing the materials. You put them between the ruler and the bench, and find out which one is best at stopping the ruler vibrating.

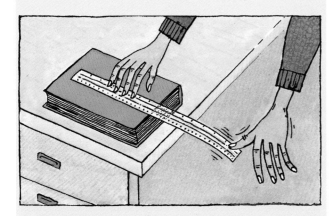

Things to think about
- How will you decide which material works best? What scoring system will you use to compare the materials?

What to do
- Carry out your tests.
- Write a report for Jo telling her what you have found out.

Reducing reverberation

Vicky has a room which is very 'echoey'. She knows that the effect is called **reverberation.** She would like to find out how to reduce it.

Investigate

Survey rooms at home and at school. Find out which rooms give strong reverberation and which features help reduce it.

Useful information
Most rooms give a slight echo when you speak. The echo comes back so quickly that you hear it before you have finished making the original sound. This effect is called reverberation.

What to do
- Carry out your survey. It might be useful to record what the walls, floors, ceilings and furnishings (carpets, curtains, furniture) are like in each room.
- What features do the 'echoey' rooms have in common?
- Write a report for Vicky telling her how you think the reverberation in her room can be reduced.

Ear defenders

The ground crew at the airport need some effective ear defenders. They would like to know the best sound insulation material to use.

Investigate

Compare different materials to find out which works best in ear defenders.

You need
Materials to test, plastic cups, items chosen by you.

Useful information
- You could make ear defenders by putting different materials inside plastic cups.
- Important! Do not use loud sounds in this investigation. They could damage your hearing.

Things to think about
- What will you use as a source of sound?
- The louder something sounds, the further away you can stand from it and still hear it. Can you make use of this idea?

What to do
- Plan and carry out your investigation.
- Write a report for the ground crew telling them which sound insulation material you recommend.

Quiet inside

Wayne wishes to insulate his house against noise. He is worried about the cost and thinks it would be sensible to test some ideas on a model first.

Investigate

Test different materials to find out which ones are best at insulating a model house against outside noises.

You need
Small cardboard box or large plastic beaker to use as a model house, materials to test, items chosen by you.

Things to think about
- What will you use as a source of sound?
- What parts of the model house will you insulate?
- How will you measure the sound level inside the model? Could you use a microphone connected to an oscilloscope?

What to do
- Plan your investigation.
- Make a list of the things you need.
- Carry out your investigation.
- Write a report for Wayne telling him what you have found out.
- Do you think that you could improve your tests? If so, how?

JANE BOND WORKS FOR THE DAILY POST. SHE IS ON A SPECIAL ASSIGNMENT, TO PHOTOGRAPH JASON CRUSH ON HIS PRIVATE ISLAND. HER NEWSPAPER SUSPECTS THAT CRUSH HAS MADE HIS FORTUNE BY FORGING BANKNOTES.

TIME TO LEAVE THE ISLAND. I HOPE THEY SEE MY SIGNAL.

JANE HAS TAKEN HER PHOTOGRAPHS.

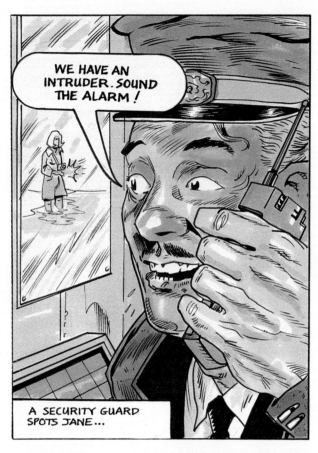

WE HAVE AN INTRUDER. SOUND THE ALARM!

A SECURITY GUARD SPOTS JANE...

MORE GUARDS SEE JANE...

I HAVE THE INTRUDER IN VIEW, BUT SHE'S ESCAPING!

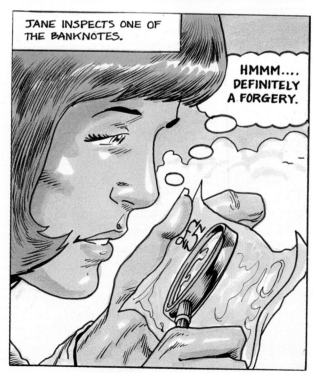

JANE INSPECTS ONE OF THE BANKNOTES.

HMMM.... DEFINITELY A FORGERY.

Light devices

The picture shows the devices that Jane and the security guards have been using. With your group, answer these questions:

1 What do you think each of the following words means?

 reflect
 image
 lens
 ray

2 What is the name of each of the devices in the picture?

3 What is each of the devices being used for in the pictures on the opposite page?

4 Which of the devices use light?

5 Which of the devices reflect light?

6 Which devices have lenses?

7 Which devices change the direction in which light travels?

8 Which devices can produce a larger-than-life image?

9 Which devices can produce a smaller-than-life image?

Jane's holiday

When Jane has finished her assignment, she goes on holiday to Blackpool. As usual, she is laden with equipment.

10 What items of equipment is Jane carrying?

11 What could Jane use each item for on her holiday?

12 Why might she need both of the cameras?

13 Write a short story called 'Jane's unexpected assignment in Blackpool'. In your story, see if you can get Jane to use all the equipment she is carrying.

Jane often wears an antique diamond ring that was given to her by her grandmother. The diamond is clear. Yet, in the light, it sparkles with many different colours.

14 What was done to the diamond to make it sparkle?

15 See if you can find out why the diamond sparkles with different colours.

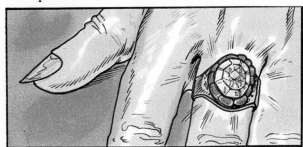

E2.2 A change of direction

Like Jane, you have been sent on an assignment. You have to report on the school science fair shown in the pictures. But there is nobody around to explain what is going on.

Investigate

- Look at the equipment in each display and read the notes left behind by the students.
- Set up each activity in your group and find out what happens.
- Write a report on each experiment explaining how it was set up and what it shows.

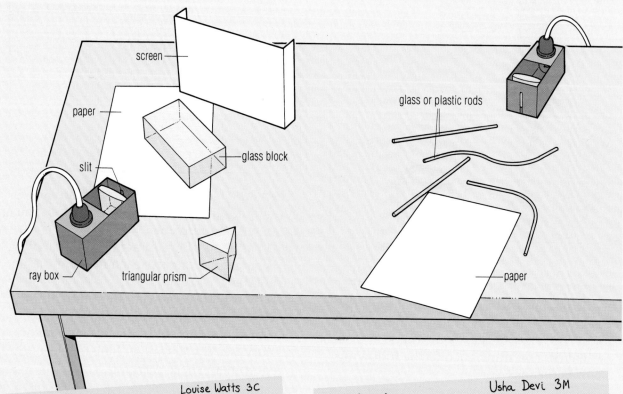

Louise Watts 3C

Prisms and blocks.
These prisms and blocks are transparent. They can bend light going in and coming out. This is called refraction. Some prisms can spread white light into all the colours of the rainbow. This is called a spectrum.

Usha Devi 3M

Optical fibres.
Optical fibres are thin strands of glass or clear plastic. They can carry light from one place to another. They are also known as light pipes. Glass or plastic rods behave in the same way.

What to do

- Shine a ray of light through each of the prisms and blocks. Which can refract the ray? Which can produce a spectrum?
- Shine a spectrum onto a white card screen. List the colours in order.
- See if you can use the inside of a prism like a mirror to reflect a ray of light.

What to do

- Shine a ray of light into one end of a glass rod. Hold a piece of white paper near the other end and see what happens.
- Try using bent glass and plastic rods.
- Why do you think that light can't escape from the sides of the rods? The prism experiments may give you some ideas.

What to do

- Use mirrors to see a pencil hidden behind one book and then two books.
- Use mirrors to reflect a ray of light round one book and then two books.
- See if you can find a way of measuring the angles at which a ray of light strikes and then leaves a mirror. How do the angles compare?

Simon Jones 3K

Seeing round corners.

Mirrors can be used to see round corners. With two mirrors you can see round two corners.

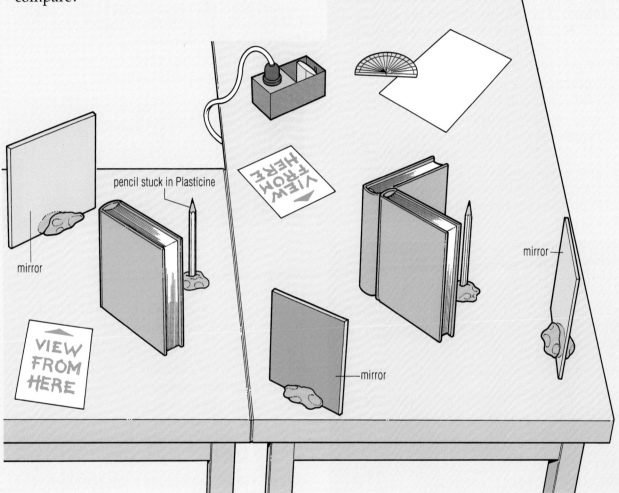

pencil stuck in Plasticine

VIEW FROM HERE

mirror

VIEW FROM HERE

mirror

mirror

After your reports...

Discuss these questions in your groups and record your answers.

1. How could mirrors be useful in a shop to help security?
2. Raindrops are rather like triangular prisms with the corners rounded off. Could this help to explain how rainbows get their colours? Describe your ideas.
3. How could small and flexible optical fibres be useful to the following: surgeons, engineers and model makers?
4. If you had an optical fibre several metres long how could you use it to send messages to a friend in another room?

E2.3 Visible and invisible

Light travels about as tiny waves, rather like ripples travelling over the surface of a pond. Light is only one member of a much bigger family of waves called the **electromagnetic spectrum**. The information on these two pages should help you answer these questions about this family.

1 Which part of the electromagnetic spectrum can our eyes see?
2 Which parts of the electromagnetic spectrum are invisible?
3 Which parts of the electromagnetic spectrum can be used for communication?
4 Which waves in the electromagnetic spectrum are the most spaced out?
5 Which waves are similar to X-rays?

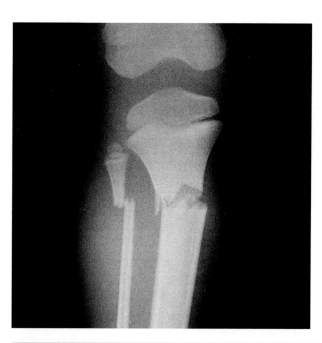

Ultraviolet (UV) waves

There are invisible UV waves in sunshine. Too much UV is harmful and can cause skin cancer. Your skin tries to shield itself against UV by making a substance called melanin. This turns your skin brown.

6 Write a short report for a newspaper on sunbathing and its dangers.

X-ray waves

X-ray waves are invisible, but some can pass right through your body! Bones allow less X-ray waves through than muscle and look lighter on an X-ray photograph.

Look at the X-ray photograph of a leg.
7 Sketch the leg in your book. Label any bones and muscles.
8 Look for the broken bones. Label the breaks on your drawing.

Did you know?

Gamma ray waves come from radioactive materials. They are similar to X-ray waves. Both types of waves are very harmful if absorbed deep in the body.

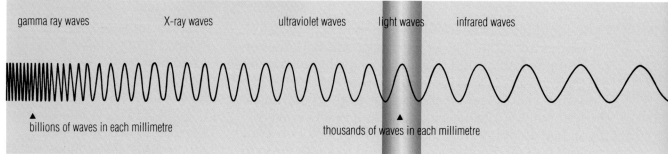

gamma ray waves   X-ray waves   ultraviolet waves   light waves   infrared waves

▲ billions of waves in each millimetre   thousands of waves in each millimetre

The electromagnetic spectrum

Infrared waves

All warm and hot things give off infrared waves, even our own bodies. The waves are invisible but you can feel their effect!

Investigate

Use the equipment in the picture to find out what effect infrared waves have and in which direction they travel.

What to do
- Boil the water in the flask.
- Turn the bunsen burner off.
- Slowly move your hand towards the flask but don't touch it. What can you feel?
- What effect do the infrared waves have?
- Draw a diagram showing the hot flask and your hand. Show the directions in which the infrared waves are travelling.

hot water

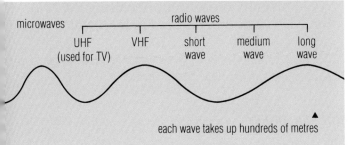

microwaves

radio waves

UHF
(used for TV)　VHF　short wave　medium wave　long wave

each wave takes up hundreds of metres

Some mystery waves

The appliance above uses waves from the electromagnetic spectrum.

9 What are the waves?
10 What is their effect on food?
11 List some things that these waves can pass through.
12 List some things that these waves cannot pass through.

Radio waves

Jane wants to know how sounds can be sent by radio. A scientist tells her that radio waves are quite different from sound waves, which are not in the electromagnetic family. However, radio waves can be used to send signals to a radio telling it what sound waves to make.

Investigate

Find out if radio waves really are different from sound waves.

Things to think about
- If you switch off a radio are radio waves still in the room?
- What materials must radio waves pass through to reach the radio?
- What materials can sound waves pass through?

What to do
- Tune a battery-powered radio in to your favourite station.
- Wrap the radio in aluminum foil. What happens to the music?
- Can you think of two possible explanations for this? What are they?
- How can you test which explanation is right?
- Carry out the test. What did you find?

E2.4 Lenses and cameras

Choosing a lens

Jane needs three types of lens for her photographic assignments: a close-up lens for showing details, a standard lens for taking pictures of larger groups or scenes, and a wide-angle lens for taking in even more of the view. But someone has muddled up her lenses. Can you sort them out for her?

Investigate

Compare the images made by the three different lenses you will be given. Decide which is best for each type of picture.

You need
White card screen, three lenses (thick, medium and thin).

What to do
- Stand well back from a sunny or brightly lit window. Hold one of the lenses between the window and the screen so that the lens is about half a metre from the screen.
- Slowly move the lens towards the screen until a clear image appears.
- Now do the same with the other lenses. Which lens gives the largest image? Which lens gives the smallest image? Which lens would you use for each type of picture?
- When you have a clear image, the distance from the lens to the screen is called the **focal length.** Measure the focal lengths of the three lenses.

Close-up shot

Standard shot

Wide-angle shot

More things to do
- When Jane found an old diary with tiny writing, she wondered if any of her lenses could magnify the writing. Try using the three lenses as magnifiers. Find out which one works best.
- Make a chart showing everything you have found out about the three lenses.

Did you know?

Lenses which are thicker in the middle than at the edge are called **convex** lenses.

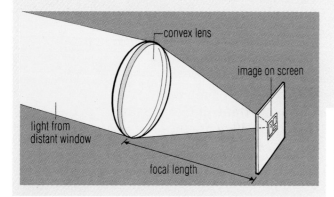

convex lens

image on screen

light from distant window

focal length

A pin-hole camera

The earliest cameras had no lenses, just a pin-hole where the lens is in a modern camera. You looked at the image on a small screen. Later, scientists discovered how to record the image so that it could be made into a photograph.

Investigate

Make a pin-hole camera and find out what images it can produce.

You need
Toilet roll tube, 2 sheets of black paper, tracing paper, aluminium foil, sticky tape, lenses used before.

What to do
- Make your pin-hole camera as shown below.
- Point your camera at a brightly lit window or bright bulb. Look at the image on the tracing paper screen. Which way up is it?
- What happens to the image if you make the pin-hole larger?
- Make the hole about 1 cm across. Put different lenses in front of the pin-hole to see which one gives the clearest image. If you use a lens instead of a pin-hole, how does this affect the brightness of the image?
- If you were going to take a photograph with the camera you have just made, where would you put the film?

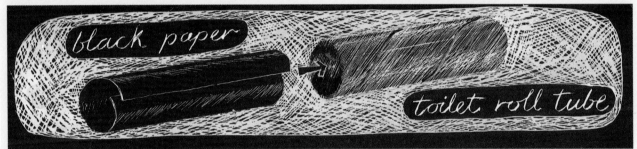

1 Cut and roll some black paper so that it exactly fits inside a toilet roll tube.

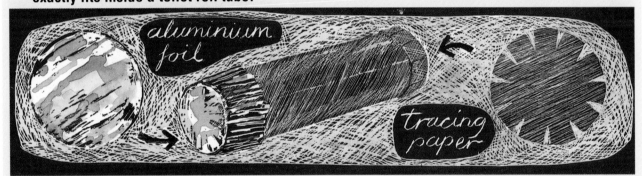

2 Use tape to fix aluminium foil over one end of the tube and tracing paper over the other.

3 Make a small hole in the aluminium foil. Then make another black paper tube to go round the tracing paper screen

E3.1 Seeing and hearing

Look at the photographs of the animals.

1 Why do you think each of these animals might need a good sense of sight or hearing?

2 Which animal do you think has the most sensitive sight? Explain your answer.

3 Which animal do you think has the most sensitive hearing? Explain your answer.

4 Which animal has the widest view? Why do you think it needs a wide view?

5 What do you think are the advantages of having two eyes facing forward?

6 People sometimes say that an eye is rather like a camera. In what ways do you think an eye is similar to a camera?

At risk

Look at the picture of the building site. It shows some people who are putting their hearing and their sight at risk.

7 What things are people doing that might damage their sight? What should they be doing to avoid this?

8 What things are people doing that might damage their hearing? What should they be doing to avoid this?

9 Phil is listening to his personal stereo on the building site. Why should he not be doing this?

Far and near

If your sight is good, you will be able to see things clearly whether they are a long way away or close to you. Your eyes automatically adjust for different distances. However, not everyone sees things so clearly.

10 Some people are 'short-sighted'. What do you think this means?

11 Some people are 'long-sighted'. What do you think this means?

12 In what ways can people who are short-sighted or long-sighted overcome their problem?

Safety!
If you are making measurements near people's eyes, they must wear goggles.

A comfortable distance

When you read a book, you normally place it so that you can see the words without straining your eyes.

13 What problems do you have if the book is too far away?

14 What problems do you have if the book is too close?

Investigate

- Carry out a survey to find how far from their eyes people prefer to hold a book so that they can read without strain. Does the result depend on whether people are short-sighted or not?

E3.2 Using your ears

Telling the direction

In the picture, Sophie looks round when she hears someone shout her name. But can she tell where the sound is coming from just by listening? And how about Mr Jones driving the car? He is having problems hearing through one ear. Will he be able to tell where the sound of a car horn is coming from? You might be able to find the answers to these questions by investigation.

Investigate

Carry out tests to find out how good people are at telling the direction of a sound. Test them when they are using both ears and then only one ear.

You need
Chalk, blindfold, cloth or ear muff to cover one ear, source of sound.

Useful information
The picture shows one way of testing how good someone is at telling the direction of a sound. The person sits blindfolded in the middle with chalk lines pointing out like spokes all around them. Someone makes a sound at the end of a spoke. The blindfolded person has to point in the direction that they think the sound is coming from.

Things to think about
* How far away from the person will you make the sound? Does it need to be the same distance each time?
* Will you go round the spokes in order or at random?
* What scoring system will you use to show how good the person is at telling the direction?
* How will you record your results?
* How many times will you carry out the test at each spoke?
* How many people will you test?
* What will you use as a source of sound?

What to do
* Plan your investigation.
* Carry out your tests.
* Find an interesting way of reporting what you have found. In your report, you could answer these questions:
Does it matter where the sound comes from? Are some people better than others at telling the direction of a sound? Does using only one ear make any difference?

Hearing aid

In the days before electronics, people sometimes used hearing trumpets if they were hard of hearing.

Investigate

Make some different shaped tubes and cones out of paper or card. Find out if these 'hearing aids' improve your hearing.

You need
Paper or card, sticky tape, source of sound (e.g. ticking stopclock), metre rule.

Things to think about
- How will you compare the different cones to find out which works best?
- If a ticking stopclock sounds louder, you don't have to stand so close to it to hear it. Can you make use of this idea in any way?
- How will you make sure that your tests are fair?

What to do
- Make your cones and tubes.
- Carry out your tests.
- Sketch the shapes that you have tried out. Describe how well they each worked. Give reasons why you think that cones and tubes might improve hearing.
- Why do you think that people sometimes cup their hands behind their ears when they are trying to hear

Concentrate!

The people in the picture are having an argument.

Investigate

- Design and carry out an experiment to try to settle their argument.

Things to think about
- If people are concentrating well, they should be able to do thinking tasks quickly and accurately. What sort of tasks will you set the people you test?
- How will you measure how well each person can concentrate? What scoring system will you use and how will you record your results.

Important! If you use personal stereos in this investigation, you must have permission from home and school. If played loud, personal stereos can damage your hearing.

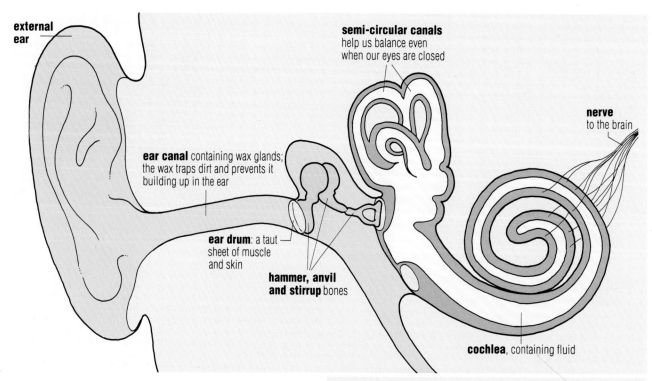

external ear

semi-circular canals help us balance even when our eyes are closed

nerve to the brain

ear canal containing wax glands; the wax traps dirt and prevents it building up in the ear

ear drum: a taut sheet of muscle and skin

hammer, anvil and stirrup bones

cochlea, containing fluid

The diagram shows the parts of the human ear.

1 Look at the diagram. Decide which parts are described by the statements below. Put the statements in the correct order to show how sounds reach the brain.

A The vibrations pass through these small bones.

B Electrical signals are sent along this to the brain

C This stretched sheet of muscle and skin vibrates when sound waves hit it.

D This picks up sound waves and funnels them into the ear canal.

E The fluid in here vibrates and the vibrations are picked up by nerve cells.

Did you know?

Old people cannot usually hear such high frequencies as young people.

Sounds which are too high for the human ear to hear are called **ultrasonic** sounds.

Hearing range

With a signal generator connected to a loud-speaker you can make a note go higher and higher until you can't hear it.

Investigate

Test your class. Find the highest notes you can all hear.

Useful information
- The **frequency** of a sound is measured in **hertz** (Hz for short). A frequency of 200 Hz means 200 sound waves every second.

What to do
- All sit quietly with your hands up.
- Listen to the sound as someone slowly turns up the frequency on the signal generator.
- As soon as you cannot hear the sound any more, put your hand down. Write down the frequency of the sound.
- Collect all the results and find an interesting way to present them.

...and the eye

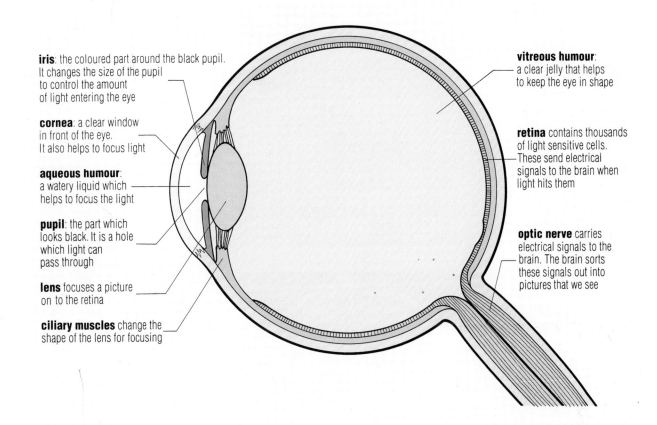

iris: the coloured part around the black pupil. It changes the size of the pupil to control the amount of light entering the eye

cornea: a clear window in front of the eye. It also helps to focus light

aqueous humour: a watery liquid which helps to focus the light

pupil: the part which looks black. It is a hole which light can pass through

lens focuses a picture on to the retina

ciliary muscles change the shape of the lens for focusing

vitreous humour: a clear jelly that helps to keep the eye in shape

retina contains thousands of light sensitive cells. These send electrical signals to the brain when light hits them

optic nerve carries electrical signals to the brain. The brain sorts these signals out into pictures that we see

The diagram above shows the parts of the human eye.

2 Which parts do the following jobs?
  a Controlling the amount of light entering the eye.
  b Focusing the light to make an image.
  c Picking up the image.
  d Keeping the eye in shape.
  e Carrying electrical signals to the brain.

3 What happens to your pupils when you walk from bright sunlight into a dark room?

The camera

A camera is rather like an eye because it focuses images onto a light-sensitive area.

4 Look at the diagrams of the camera and the eye. Make a table with two columns to show the parts of the eye and the camera which do similar jobs.

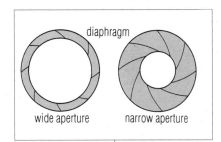

diaphragm

wide aperture   narrow aperture

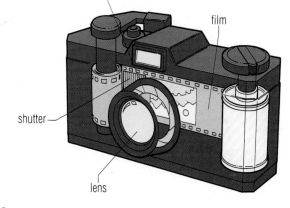

film

shutter

lens

Camera

E3.4 Eye problems

A

B

I am short sighted. I can read all right without my glasses, but distant things look blurred.

I am long sighted. I can see distant things all right, but I can't read without my glasses.

Tim and Liz both have sight defects. The pictures show you what they see, but you have to work out which view is which.

1 Which picture shows Liz's view without glasses?
2 Give some examples of the problems Tim and Liz might have if they forget to wear their glasses.

Did you know?

Convex lenses are thicker in the middle than at the edge.
Concave lenses are thinner in the middle than at the edge.
Both types of lenses are used in spectacles. They are curved to follow the shape of the eye.

3 Check in your class to see if people with glasses have concave or convex lenses in them. Remember: you must handle spectacles very carefully!
4 Look through both types of lens. How do they compare?

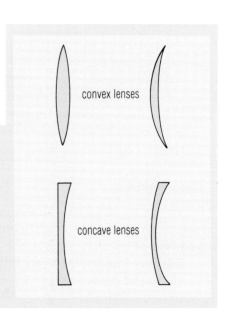

convex lenses

concave lenses

Lenses at work

Lenses bend light rather like prisms. But lenses are specially shaped so that the bending of the rays is carefully controlled. Some lenses try to spread rays further apart. Others try to bring them closer together. You can see this on the right. If the rays meet, scientists say that they are **focused**.

5 What does a concave lens do to light rays?

6 What does a convex lens do to light rays?

The eye lens can change shape. It is naturally stretched thin, but there are muscles in the eye which can make the lens fatter.

7 If the eye lens becomes fatter, how will this change what it does to the rays?

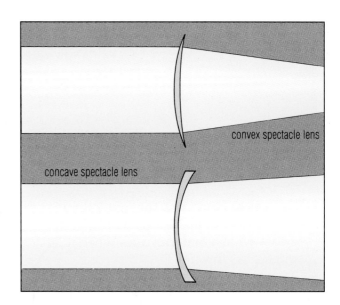

convex spectacle lens

concave spectacle lens

Tim's problem

Tim's eye lens cannot become thin enough for looking at distant things. The rays are brought together too much. They cross before they reach the retina. By the time they reach the retina, they have started to spread again.

8 Tim needs a spectacle lens that will spread the rays a little before they enter his eye. What sort of lens does he need, convex or concave?

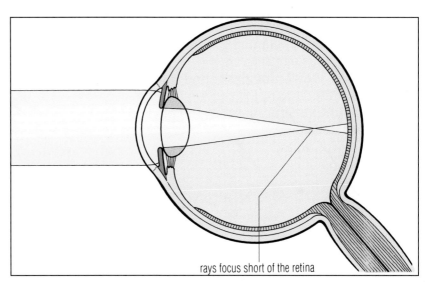

rays focus short of the retina

Short-sighted eye

Liz's problem

Liz's eye lens cannot become fat enough for looking at close things. It doesn't bring the rays together enough, so they have still not met when they reach the retina.

9 Where would the rays focus in Liz's eye if the retina was not there?

10 Liz needs a spectacle lens that will start to bring the rays together before they enter her eye. What sort of lens does she need, convex or concave?

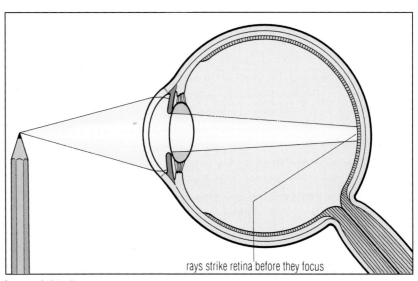

rays strike retina before they focus

Long-sighted eye

Stepping stones

Soundword

1	2	3	4	5	6	7	8	9

1 Solve these clues. Use the first letter of each answer to make a word which describes what a material does when it lets sound pass through.

1. Line on an oscilloscope screen.
2. What a hard surface does to sound waves.
3. Height of a wave peak.
4. Annoying, unwanted sound.
5. What your ear detects.
6. Device which changes sound into electrical signals.
7. If the frequency does this, the pitch goes up.
8. Series of notes.
9. It is about 330 m/s in air.

Lightword

1	2	3	4	5	6	7	8	9

2 Solve these clues. Use the first letter of each answer to make the name of a device which lets you see over the top of things.

1. Type of glass or plastic block.
2. Part of the body which detects light.
3. What a glass block does to light.
4. Controls the amount of light entering the eye.
5. Range of colours from a prism.
6. Lens which is thickest in the middle.
7. Glass strand which can transmit light.
8. Dark part in the middle of the eye.
9. Light is a member of this family of waves.

A question of lenses

This is what Dave looks like with and without his glasses.

3. What type of lenses do you think Dave has in his glasses?
   Are his lenses thickest in the middle or round the edge?
4. Is Dave long-sighted or short-sighted? What problems do you think he has when looking at things without his glasses?

Model camera

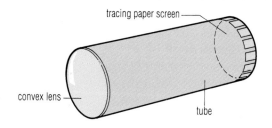

tracing paper screen

convex lens

tube

Rachel has made a model to show how the image is formed in a camera. It is a cardboard tube with a lens at one end and a piece of tracing paper over the other.

5. What changes should she make to her model if she wants to use a fatter lens?
6. How would the image then be different from the one before?

Sounds different

Dave reckons that his cassette player sounds different when he listens to it in his kitchen instead of his bedroom.

7 In what way do you think his cassette player might sound different?

8 What is the effect called? How would you explain it to Dave?

Dave lives close to Stansgate Airport.

9 Design a leaflet for Dave and the other residents, giving them hints on how they can insulate their homes against noise and reduce vibrations.

Sound changes

These are the wave traces Rachel got when she used an oscilloscope to study four different sounds.

10 What did Rachel connect to the oscilloscope to get the traces?

11 Which wave trace had the greatest amplitude?

12 Which sound had the highest frequency?

13 Which sound had the highest pitch?

14 Which was loudest?

Sound A   Sound B

Sound C   Sound D

Wave mix-up

Dave watched a TV programme about electromagnetic waves. He took some notes on a piece of scrap paper. Now he can't work out which comment goes with which type of wave. Can you sort his notes?

15 One type of wave shouldn't be there at all. Which one?

16 Put the rest of the waves in a list. They should be in order, with the most spaced out waves at the top and the least spaced out at the bottom.

17 Alongside each type of wave, put the comment that you think Dave meant to write there.

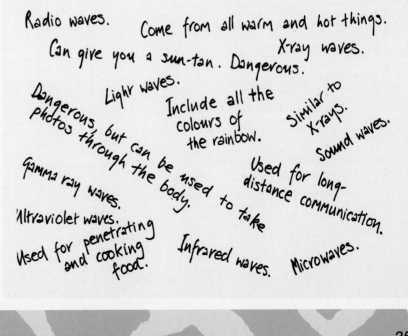

Radio waves. Come from all warm and hot things. Can give you a sun-tan. Dangerous. X-ray waves. Light waves. Include all the colours of the rainbow. Similar to X-rays. Sound waves. Dangerous but can be used to take photos through the body. Used for long-distance communication. Gamma ray waves. Ultraviolet waves. Used for penetrating and cooking food. Infrared waves. Microwaves.

OXFORD
SCIENCE
programme

E   The active Earth

F1.1 Weather everywhere

Yachting is a very popular sport. But it can be dangerous in bad weather conditions.

1 Why is the wind speed and direction important?

2 Why do you think sea-going yachts carry radio transmitters and receivers?

3 What sort of information is given in the shipping forecasts on the radio?

Fell walking and climbing can be miserable and dangerous in the wrong weather conditions.

4 What weather conditions do you think are particularly dangerous in the hills?

5 What information would you expect the local weather information services to give?

Farmers are very dependent on the weather particularly at harvest time.

6 What sort of weather is needed at harvest?

7 What sort of weather do farmers want while the crops are growing?

8 Why do you think farmers have their own weather service on the radio?

There are many other groups of people who need their own special weather forecasts.

9 How many can you think of? Make a list.

Studying the weather

Anil wants to find out how different kinds of weather happen. Sarah wants to be able to record the weather.

10 In your group, discuss all the things Anil and Sarah might study to investigate the weather. The satellite picture of the British Isles may give you some ideas. One way to make a summary of your ideas is to have a brainstorming session like this:

- Get a large sheet of paper and a felt-tip pen.
- Choose someone to be the writer.
- Write WEATHER in the middle of your sheet.
- Get the writer to jot down your ideas all over the sheet at any angle. Make each idea only one or two words long.
- Compare your sheet with the other groups.

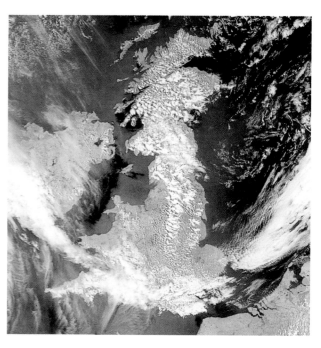

Weather and water

The picture on the right shows different weather conditions over the sea and the land. Discuss and answer these questions with your group:

11 What is forming over the sea?

12 Why is this happening?

13 Where are the clouds moving?

14 What is happening over the hills?

15 Where does the rain water go?

16 Imagine you are a tiny particle of water in the picture. Describe your travels.

Charting the weather

Weather forecasters often make charts like the one on the right.

17 What symbols tell you that rain is likely?

18 How are clouds shown?

19 How are winds shown?

20 What shows fine weather?

21 What shows cold or warm weather?

22 How are thunderstorms shown?

Catastrophic weather

The newspaper headlines show some of the problems that weather can bring. With your group:

23 Make a list of the catastrophic weather events that can happen around the world.

24 Classify these events into long-term problems and short-term problems.

25 Write a letter to a friend abroad describing an unusual and dangerous weather event in your own country.

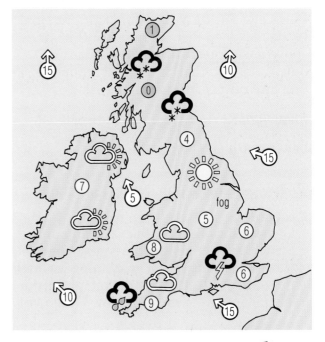

BIG FREEZE UP

FLOOD DEVASTATES

CROPS FAIL IN DROUGHT

HURRICANE H

Did you know?

The study of weather is called **meteorology**. Scientists who study and forecast the weather are called **meteorologists**.

On weather maps or charts there are lines, numbers and words that tell you about the air pressure in different places. In your group, look at the weather map and see if you can answer these questions.

1. Where is the air pressure high?
2. Where is the air pressure low?
3. What sort of weather do we often get when the pressure is high?
4. What sort of weather do we often get when the pressure is low?
5. How do we know from the map when two places have the same air pressure?

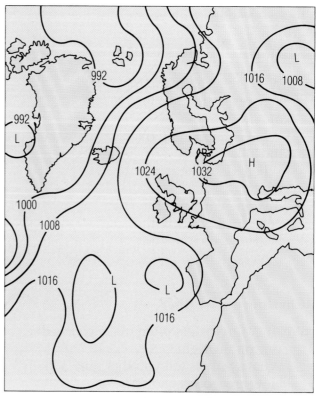

Where does air press?

Linda and Sue disagreed about air pressure. Linda reckoned that, as there is lots of air above us, its pressure tends to squash us down. Sue said that, as air is all around us, its pressure pushes in from all directions.

Investigate

Find out who is right, Linda or Sue.

You need
Empty oil can, vacuum pump for removing air.

What to do
- Connect the oil can to the vacuum pump.
- Switch on after getting the connection checked.
- When the pump has been running for a while, where is the pressure greatest, inside the can or outside?
- What happens to the can? How would you explain this?

Air in balloons

Linda was blowing up balloons and then letting them down. She wondered whether the air rushed out quickly because it was at a higher pressure than the air outside.

Investigate

You can measure the pressure of the air in a balloon with a **Bourdon gauge** like the one in the picture.
- Measure the pressure in a balloon.
- Could differences in pressure cause winds? Discuss your ideas in your group.

Bourdon gauge

Did you know?

We live at the bottom of an ocean of air called the atmosphere. It contains 560 million million tonnes of air and is over 80 kilometres deep.

Damp camping

Linda and Sue noticed that, in the early morning, the outside of their tent was wet even though it hadn't rained. However, the tent soon dried out. Linda thought that this might be because of the wind. Sue wondered if the warmth of the Sun was drying the tent. Perhaps they were both right!

Investigate

Find out what things can make a wet material dry more quickly.

Things to think about
- How are you going to make your tests fair?
- What are you going to change in each test?

What to do
- Make a list of the things you need
- Plan and carry out your tests.
- Compare your findings with other groups.
- What do you think happens to the water in a material which dries out?

When Linda and Sue had iced drinks at a cafe, they noticed that drops of water collected on the outside of their glasses. Linda reckoned that water vapour in the air was condensing on the glass because it was cold.

Investigate

Find out if water vapour condenses best on a warm or cold surface.

Things to think about
- How can you make sure there is lots of water vapour around?
- How are you going to get a really cold, dry surface?

What to do
- Make a list of the things you need.
- With your group, plan and carry out your tests.
- Was Linda right? Make a report on what you did and what you found out.
- Explain why you think the tent got wet in the night.

Linda's drink

Clouds, fog, frost and dew.

Whenever the temperature falls, water vapour can condense into tiny drops of water. If it is cold enough, tiny ice crystals can form. Clouds are just millions of tiny water droplets or ice crystals floating about in the air.

6 How do you think fog is formed?
7 How do you think we get frost?
8 How do you think dew is formed?

Frost on window

F1.3 Recording the weather

Recording the wind

Look at the picture on the right.
1 What is the weather vane showing?
2 The other device is an **anemometer**. What do you think it is measuring?

Investigate

Design, make and use your own devices for measuring wind speed and direction.

You may need
Card, balsa wood, nails, glue, yoghurt pots, stop clock, compass.

Things to think about
- How will you record which way your weather vane is pointing?
- What scale will you use for measuring wind speed? Could you use the **Beaufort numbers** shown in the table?
- How will you estimate the wind speed from your measurements?

What to do
- Plan and draw your designs.
- Check your designs with your teacher.
- Make and try out your designs.
- Keep a record of your measurements for a week.

Recording temperature

Weather stations contain several instruments to record the weather. One of them is a **maximum** and **minimum thermometer**. This records the highest and lowest temperatures reached each day.
3 Why do you think the thermometer is kept in the shade?

Investigate

- Keep records of how the outside temperature varies. If you have no special thermometer, measure the temperature in the shade at the same time each day for a week.

0	Calm	smoke vertical
1	Light air	smoke moves
2	Slight breeze	leaves rustle
3	Gentle breeze	twigs move
4	Moderate breeze	branches move
5	Fresh breeze	small trees sway
6	Strong breeze	large branches move
7	Near gale	large trees sway
8	Gale	twigs break off
9	Severe gale	tiles blown off
10	Storm	trees uprooted
11	Violent storm	widespread damage
12	Hurricane	countryside devastated

The Beaufort scale

Records and forecasts

You can keep weather records in a school and use them to produce your own forecasts.

Investigate

Make a weather chart to go up in the school each day. Try using your records to forecast the next day's weather.

Useful information
You can measure daily rainfall with a rain gauge and air pressure with a barometer.

Things to think about
* What information are you going to record?
* How can you change or add information?
* In your group, who is going to do what each day?

What to do
* Design and make your weather chart.
* Keep your weather records for at least a week.
* Try producing your own forecasts.
* Keep a record of your predictions and see how many were right during a week and how many were wrong!
* Over the week, collect examples of weather maps and weather satellite photographs. Watch the television weather forecasts and see if they are right!

Fronts

Scientists call the meeting point between a mass of warm air and a mass of cold air a **front**. A front brings weather changes.

4 What changes would you see as the fronts in the chart move across the country from west to east?

When a mass of warm air is moving towards and over a mass of cold air, the boundary is called a warm front. When a mass of cold air is moving towards and under a mass of warm air, the boundary is called a cold front. You can see the symbols used for warm and cold fronts on the right.

5 With your group, study weather maps and forecasts in newspapers and on TV to find out what sorts of weather are produced by the different fronts.

Collecting and measuring the water from a rain gauge.

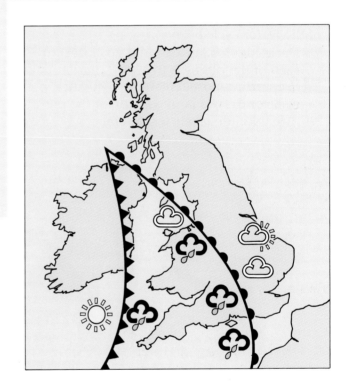

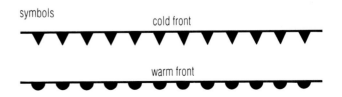
symbols cold front warm front

F1.4 Weather and water

With your group, decide what answers you would give to a friend who asks you these questions:

1 Where does all the rain go when the ground dries out?

2 Why does the atmosphere never run out of rain?

The water cycle

The Earth's water is never used up because the rain falling to the ground is replaced by water evaporating back into the atmosphere. This is called the **water cycle**.

The labels on the right belong on the picture of the water cycle below.

3 Decide which label should go closest to each of the places A to L.

4 Prepare a report explaining the water cycle or draw a large version of the picture with the labels written in.

Clouds lose water as rain
Water vapour condenses to form clouds
River flows to the sea
Water goes into a reservoir
Wind blows clouds towards the land
Rain runs into streams
Streams flow into river
Water piped to factories and houses
Water from sewage returned to sea
Water evaporates from sea
Water evaporates from plants and trees
Water seeps through ground

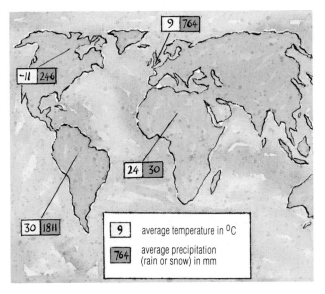

The type of weather a country gets over a long period of time is called its climate. For example, Britain has a mild **climate**. Rarely is it too hot or too cold.

5 Look at the photographs A,B,C and D. Describe the climate in each one.

6 Discuss the problems of living in each of the climates. You may wish to consider people's clothing or types of houses.

7 Look at the world map above. Study the data about annual rainfall and temperature. Decide which of the four places you think each of the photographs shows.

8 Draw weather symbols for the weather in each photograph.

Changed by the weather

The weather does not only affect the plants and animals on Earth. Rocks and buildings may also be changed.

9 How has the weather affected any rocks or stone you can see in the photographs?

10 How do you think this happened?

11 Make a list of things near your school that have been changed by the weather.

Different weather

45

F2.1 Making landscapes

The surfaces of things can often be changed.
Look at the photographs on this page and
answer these questions with your group:

1 What has caused the surface damage
  shown in each photograph?
2 Could the damage have been stopped? If
  so, how?

Outdoors, the surface of a material can be
weakened by the action of the weather. This
is called **weathering**. For example, rain is
slightly acid and can dissolve some types of
rock. This is known as chemical weathering.

3 Can you see any examples of chemical
  weathering in the photographs? If so,
  where?
4 How else can weather weaken a surface?

Once a surface has been weakened, it can be
worn away. The wearing away of a surface is
called **erosion**.

5 List some of the things that could erode
  (wear away) a surface.
6 Can you think of some examples where
  erosion might be useful? Make a list.
7 Carry out a survey of weathered and
  eroded materials in your area. Decide how
  you think each material was weathered or
  eroded.

Eroded landscapes

The wearing away of rocks on a large scale can cause big changes to the surface of the Earth. Look at the photographs on this page and then answer these questions with your group.

8 How has erosion changed each land-scape?

9 Why do you think some of the rocks have been eroded more than others?

Headlands and bays

The map shows how the sea has eroded the coast in one part of South-East Dorset. Some of the rock types are shown. Next to each is a description of the rock.

10 Why is there a headland at Ballard Point?

11 Why is there a bay at Studland Bay?

12 What type of rock do you think might be found at Swanage Bay?

13 Draw the coastline as it might look in a few thousand years time.

The bays have been formed because frag-ments of rock have been broken away from the cliffs and carried away. The process is still going on.

14 What carries the fragments away?

15 Where do you think the fragments go?

16 What do you think happens to the rock fragments at the end of their journey?

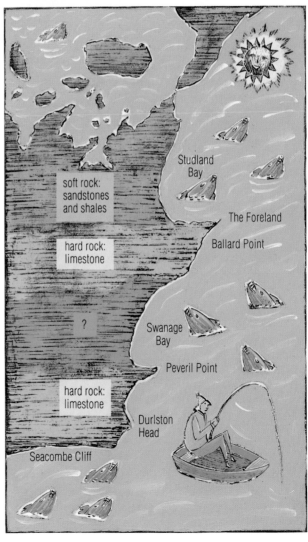

soft rock: sandstones and shales

hard rock: limestone

hard rock: limestone

Studland Bay

The Foreland

Ballard Point

?

Swanage Bay

Peveril Point

Durlston Head

Seacombe Cliff

F2.2 Wearing away

The pictures show some examples of erosion.
1. What has happened in each case?
2. What was the cause of the problem?
3. What do you think has happened to all the material worn away?

Lots of materials found at home, at school and in machines can become worn away with use.
4. What examples can you think of?

Step test

It took hundreds of years for the steps in the photograph to be eroded. Some materials would have worn away more quickly.

Investigate

Find the best material to be used for the steps leading to a new block of classrooms.

You need
Samples of stone, rock or other materials, items chosen by you.

Things to think about
- How can you wear away your samples quickly? Using your feet would take too long!
- How will you measure the wear?
- Will your tests be fair?

What to do
- Plan your investigation and list the equipment you need.
- Ask your teacher to check your plan.
- Carry out the investigation.
- Record all of your findings.
- Make a report of your findings.
- Could your tests have been improved? If so, how?

More things to do
- Study the steps used in your school. Look for any features they have which are designed to reduce wear.

Rivers at work

Running water can wear away rocks and soil.
Look at the photographs above.

5 Which river will do the most damage
along the bank? Why?

Investigate

Use a sand tray like the one in the diagram to
find out if fast water wears away sand more
quickly than slow water.

You need
Sand tray, sand, rubber tubing, plastic dish,
stopwatch or clock.

Things to think about
- How will you set the flow of water?
- For how long will you run each test?
- How will you measure the amount of
  erosion?
- How will you make sure that your tests are
  fair?
- What will you need to record?

What to do
- Set up the sand tray.
- Carry out your tests.
- Prepare a report on what you have found.
- What happens to the sand carried away by
  the water?

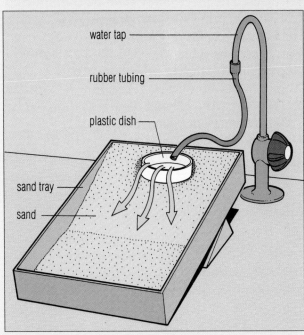

**Important! In carrying out this investigation, you must make
sure that sand does not get into the sink.**

Useful information
- The volume of water flowing over the sand
  can be controlled by the tap.
- A steeper slope will make the water flow
  faster.

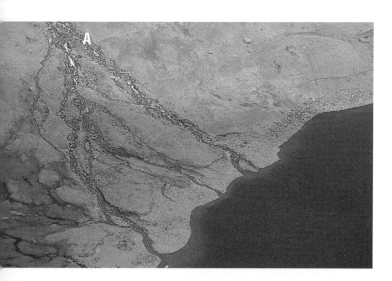

Weathering will break rocks down into pieces, some so small that they are just tiny particles. The pieces may then be **transported** (carried) to other places. Sometimes they may not move very far. For example, **scree** is pieces of rock which have broken off a mountainside and fallen in piles beneath it.

Look at the photographs A to D.

1. What materials have been transported?
2. How has each been transported?
3. Could the materials move any further?
4. Which photograph shows mountain scree?

Deposited particles

When pieces of rock can be transported no further, they settle. Scientists say they have been **deposited**. Eventually these deposits may become squashed together to form new, hard rocks.

Investigate

Use a sand tray to find out how different sized particles are deposited by water.

What to do
- Mix pebbles, sand, stones and chalk.
- Add the mixture to the sand tray.
- Let the water flow over the mixture.
- Report on your findings.

You need
Sand tray as shown in spread F2.2, sand, pebbles, chalk, a few large stones, rubber tubing, plastic dish.

Useful information
A slow flow rate will allow different types of particle to settle in different positions.

From sea, desert or mountain?

Rocks E and F in the photograph are called **sandstones**. One was formed from particles deposited in a hot, dry desert. The other was formed from particles deposited in a sea.

5 List as many features as you can about the rocks. Which features do you think could have been caused by desert conditions and which by water?

6 Which of the rocks do you think was formed from particles deposited underwater?

There are other questions that are useful when studying rock deposits:

Are the fragments large or small?
Are the fragments round or jagged?
Are there any layers?

Rounded fragments have usually been in water for a long time. Layers are also evidence that the deposits once settled in water. Look at rocks G and H in the photograph.

7 Which rock was once a beach deposit?

8 Which was formed from mountain scree?

Red sandstone

Cretaceous sandstone

Conglomerate

Breccia

Particles in soils

Soil contains many different particles (tiny fragments) which have been eroded from the rock underneath.

Investigate

Find out what particles there are in some samples of soil.

You need
Soil samples, newspaper, hand lens, gas jar, water, spatula.

Useful information
When soil is mixed with water, its particles will settle at different rates into layers.

What to do
- Try to separate and identify the different particles in a sample of soil.
- Mix some soil and water in a gas jar. You need about three times as much water as soil. Wait for the particles to settle. Draw the layers which form.
- Compare results from different soil samples. Make a poster to show your findings.

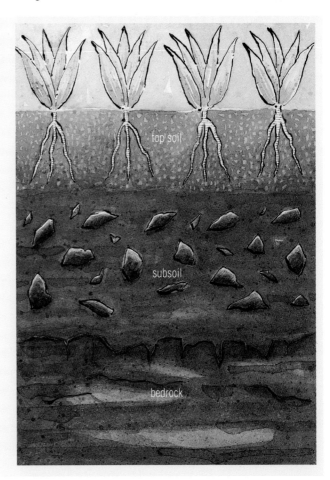

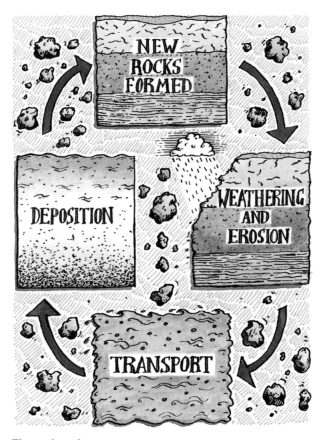

The rock cycle

The chart shows how rocks are formed, broken down, moved and reformed over and over again. It is called the **rock cycle**.

Look at photographs A, B and C.

1 Which photographs show rock being eroded?

2 In which photographs are small fragments of rock being transported?

3 Which photographs show where small pieces of rock are being deposited?

It can take a long time for small pieces of rock to be eroded from a surface, transported to another place and then deposited. It can take millions of years for the small pieces to be compacted together and changed into hard rock.

4 Describe the changes that one such particle might see during its journey round the cycle.

People problems in Cragland

Number visiting park (in thousands)	1986	1987	1988	1989	1990
People	300	420	480	520	600
Cars	60	90	100	120	200
Heavy lorries	10	12	16	20	25

Causes of erosion by people	Damage (in thousands of pounds)		
	1988	1989	1990
Not closing gates	6	6	6
Not keeping to paths	24	29	30
Breaking down walls	4	5	6
Breaking down fences	7	3	9
Careless parking	3	2	2
Overuse by walkers	69	82	90
Vandalism	1	1	1

Cragland is an area of great natural beauty. Many people visit it and walk in the hills. Imagine that you have to plan a campaign to reduce erosion caused by visitors. Look at the tables of data prepared at the end of 1989.

5 How many more people visited Cragland in 1989 than in 1986?

6 Make your own estimate of the number of visitors for 1991.

7 List the three main ways in which people caused erosion problems in 1989.

8 How might controlling traffic reduce erosion?

The areas thought to be most in danger from human erosion are Bowbells Valley, Upper Style Shoulder and Eldonwater.

9 Draw up a list of actions that you think should be taken to reduce the erosion problems caused by people in the three areas at risk.

10 Make a poster or leaflet advertising your decisions.

Useful rock deposits

Look at the picture on the right. It shows a deposit made from tiny pieces of rock.

11 How is the deposit being put to use?

12 What other uses does this deposit have?

13 Where did the rock pieces come from?

14 How many other useful rock deposits can you think of? Make a list.

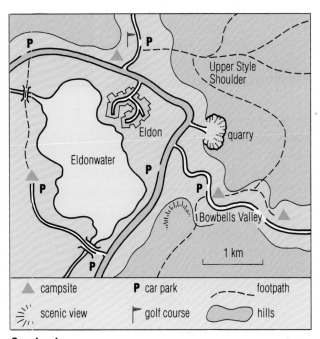

▲ campsite	**P** car park · · · · footpath
scenic view	golf course ⬭ hills

Cragland

Rocks have many important uses. Some of these uses are shown in the photograph. With your group:

1 Make a list of all the ways in which rocks, or the materials in them, can be used.

The ways in which a material behaves are called its **properties**. Here are some questions that could be asked about the properties of a material:

How hard is the material?
How shiny is the material?
Is the material brittle?

2 Think of some other questions about the properties of a material. What are they?

3 List three important properties that make rocks so useful.

Rocks are made from materials called **minerals**. Often, these are in regular shapes called **crystals**. Some are very valuable. Answer the following with your group:

4 Describe one way in which each of the minerals in the photograph is different from the rest.

5 See if you can find out what any of these minerals are used for.

Minerals

a Quartz
b Fluorite
c Pyrite
d Calcite
e Garnet
f Sphalerite
g Hematite
h Malachite
i Hornblende
j Asbestos
k Cassiterite
l Amethyst
m Barite
n Mica

Heavier or not?

Terry reckons that one property of rock is that it is much heavier than wood. But is it? The people in the picture on the right certainly don't think so.

6 Can you think of a fair way of comparing rocks and other materials by weighing? What would it be?

Hot rocks.

Imagine that you are on holiday with your group on an island. There is a volcano on the island. For years it was dormant but now it has become active and has started to erupt.

7 Why is the volcano shaped like a cone?
8 What things will be coming out of the erupting volcano?
9 What are the dangers to people and houses on the island?
10 What action should be taken to help the people on the island?

When you have discussed these with your group:

11 Report your ideas to the rest of the class.

Homes threatened by molten lava from volcano

Kiri and Nico are visiting a volcanic island. They have made some interesting observations which you can see in the picture above. With your group:

12 If you were on the island, what would you tell Kiri and Nico about how the rocks could have been formed?

F3.2 Volcanoes and earthquakes

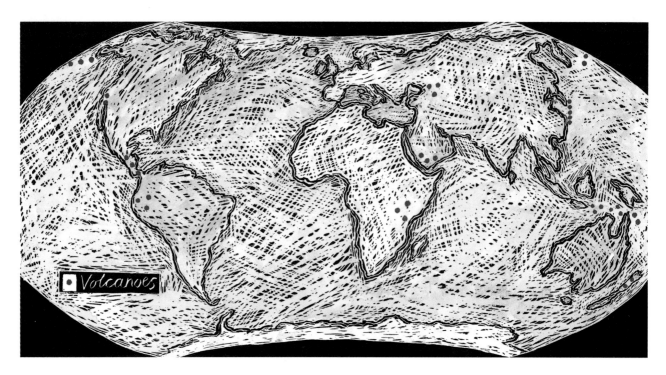

Miranda thinks that volcanoes only occur in certain parts of the world. To test her ideas she studied a map which had dots to show where the volcanoes were.

1 Do you agree with her? Do you think a regular pattern can be seen in the map above?

There are still some volcanoes that have not been placed on the map. With your group:

2 Look at the list of volcanoes and find out where they are. Use an atlas to help you.

3 See if the volcanoes fit into the pattern above. It might help to trace the map and mark the volcanoes on your drawing.

4 Prepare a report that explains where volcanoes are found.

Stewart wonders if earthquakes are found in the same areas as volcanoes. You can try out this idea for him.

5 Look at the list of earthquakes. Use an atlas to find out where they are.

6 See if the earthquakes fit the same pattern as the volcanoes. It might help to mark the earthquakes on your tracing.

7 Prepare a report on what you have found.

8 Find out about some earthquakes not given in the list.

Scientists think that the Earth's outer layer is made up of several large pieces called **plates** which slowly move relative to one another. Earthquakes and volcanoes tend to occur along the joins between the pieces.

Volcanoes:

Krakatoa, Java
Mt. Katmai, Alaska
Vesuvius, Italy
Mt. St. Helens, USA
Mauna Loa, Hawaii
Tongariro, New Zealand
Fujiyama, Japan

Earthquakes:

San Francisco (1906, 1989)
Agadir, Morocco (1960)
Anchorage, Alaska (1964)
Bogota, Colombia (1967)
Mexico City, Mexico (1970)
El Asnam, Algeria (1980)
Armenia, USSR (1989)
N. Australia (1989)

Inside volcanoes

There are many types of volcanoes. Some have steep-sided cones. Others are much flatter and wider. For example the volcanoes of Hawaii have bases nearly 100 kilometres across. Many volcanoes have the structure shown in the diagram on the right. With your group:

9 Study the labels below the diagram. Decide which label should go with each letter on the diagram.

10 Draw a larger version of the diagram with a different shape of volcano.

Molten rock from a volcano is called **lava**. The lava from some volcanoes is very runny. From others, it hardly flows at all. It is very **viscous**. When lava cools, it turns solid. The height of a volcano can increase as more and more lava turns solid. Some volcanoes send out clouds of ash and 'bombs' of gas-filled lava. Bubbles of gas become trapped in the lava when it cools and a rock called **pumice** is formed.

11 Which materials would you expect to form a high volcano?

12 Which materials would form a flatter volcano?

13 Find out what pumice is used for.

Labels for diagram:
 clouds of ash, steam and gas
 hot, liquid lava flowing down cone
 volcanic 'bombs' thrown out
 molten magma chamber
 cone made up of layers of lava and ash

Earthquake-proof

In earthquake areas, buildings have to be specially designed to withstand the shocks.

Investigate

Design a model of a structure that can withstand earthquakes. Your model should be able to support a 2 kg mass 20 cm above the ground.

You need
15 straws, 4 pipe-cleaners, thin card, 2 kg mass, scissors, sticky tape.

What to do
- Plan your structure. Ask your teacher to check your plan.
- Build and test your structure.
- Prepare a report on your structure. Mention its special features and how it performed in your tests.

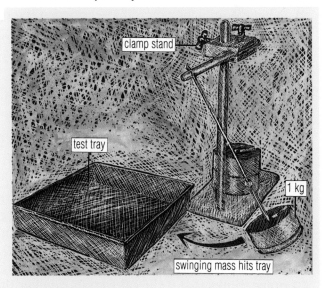

Useful information
- The diagram above shows one way of testing your model.
- Earthquakes shake buildings up and down as well as side to side.
- Pipe-cleaners can be used to join straws.

F3.3 Making rocks

Made by cooling

Granite

Microgranite

Basalt

The rocks in the photographs were all formed from **molten** (melted) materials in the Earth. When these cooled, they turned into solid rock. Rocks made in this way are called **igneous** rocks.

1 What differences can you see between the rocks in the photographs above?

Investigate

Find out what happens when a molten material cools.

You need
Bunsen burner, tripod, hand lens, salol, water, microscope slide.

What to do
- Use gentle heat to melt some salol on a microscope slide. A safe way of doing this is shown in the picture.
- When the salol has cooled and solidified, study it with a lens.
- Record your findings.
- Louise thinks that if the salol cools quicker the crystals will be smaller. Plan a fair test to check her idea.
- Carry out the test and record your findings. Do you agree with Louise?

Look again at the photographs at the top of the page.
2 Why do you think the rocks have different crystal sizes?

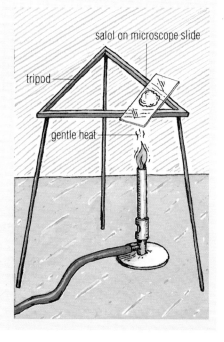

Made from fragments?

Obsidian

Conglomerate

Shelly limestone

Not all rocks are formed from molten material. Many are made from fragments of other rocks or shells. Look at the rocks in the photographs above.

3 Which have been made from fragments?

4 Why do you think some of the fragments are smooth and rounded? Where might they have come from?

5 How are the fragments held together?

6 Can you think of any artificial materials which are made by mixing small fragments together? What are they?

Investigate

Find out how a mixture of fragments settles in water.

You need
Rock fragments (soil, gravel, sand, pebbles), tall jar, stirrer, water.

What to do
- Mix the fragments together.
- Add the mixture to water in a tall jar. The diagram shows you how.
- Leave the fragments to settle. Complete settling may take several days!
- Record how the fragments have settled.
- Could the results of your investigation help explain how any of the rocks in the photographs might have been formed? If so, how?

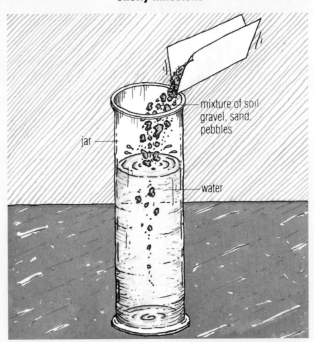

mixture of soil gravel, sand, pebbles

jar

water

Rocks made from fragments which have settled are called **sedimentary** rocks. They can form in oceans, rivers, lakes and deserts. Bits of shells, plants, and bones from dead animals can be buried with rock fragments and preserved as **fossils**. These can give clues about the age of the rocks and the climate at the time.

7 If a rock had fossilized coral in it, what would this tell you about the climate when the rock started to form?

8 Why do you think fossils are not found in igneous rocks?

F3.4 Testing rocks and minerals

Best for the job

Rocks can be cut and smoothed and used to cover the fronts of buildings.

Investigate

Test some rock samples to see which is best as the decorative front to a building.

Useful information
- The material should be strong and attractive. It should not easily break into flakes or grains.
- Hard rock will scratch soft rock.
- Rain is slightly acid and will dissolve some rocks.
- To test the strength of a rock, you could try crushing it with a G-clamp.
- *If you are crushing rock or using acid , you must wear safety goggles.*

Things to think about
- What properties will you test?
- How will you compare the rocks in each test?

You need

Rock samples, goggles, items chosen by you.

What to do
- Plan your investigation.
- Ask your teacher to check your plan.
- Carry out your tests. Record your results.
- Which material was most suitable? Prepare a report explaining your choice.

Mineral	Colour	Hardness	Streak	Shape or form	Lustre	In acid
Calcite	white	3	white	crystals	shiny	fizzes
Quartz	clear	7	white	crystals	shiny	-
Fluorite	varies	4	white	crystals	shiny	dissolves in sulphuric
Gypsum	white	2	white	crystals	dull	-
Mica	white or black	2.5	white	crystals form sheets	shiny	-
Galena	grey	2.5	grey	crystals	metallic	-
Malachite	green	3.5 - 4.0	green	rounded, banded	dull	fizzes
Hematite	black and brown	5.5	red	rounded	metallic	-

Some minerals and their properties

Mineral hunt

You have to investigate the theft of a specimen of calcite from a museum. Several minerals have been found. You must carry out tests to see if the calcite is amongst them. There is a table of information about different minerals on the opposite page.

Investigate

Test the mineral samples and identify the calcite.

You need
Mineral samples, dilute acids (hydrochloric and sulphuric), beakers, droppers, board, materials for scratch tests: 2p coin, piece of glass, steel nail, unglazed tile.

What to do
- Plan your investigation.
- Test the mineral samples.
- Record your findings. Which mineral was the stolen one?
- See if you can identify any of the other minerals.

Useful information
- If you scratch a mineral on something harder, it leaves a trail of a fine powder. The colour is called the **streak**.
- The **lustre** of a mineral tells you how its surface looks in the light.
- The hardness of a mineral is measured on the **Mohs scale**:

10	Hard as diamond
9	Will
8	scratch
7	glass
6	Scratched by quartz
5	Scratched by steel nail
4	Scratched by glass
3	Scratched by iron nail
2	Scratched by coin
1	Soft as talc, crushed by finger

Density check

The **density** of a material tells you the number of grams packed into every centimetre cubed. For example, quartz has a density of 2.7g/cm³. It has 2.7 grams of mass in each centimetre cubed of its volume. Measuring density is another way of helping you identify a mineral.

Investigate

Use some density measurements to check the results of the previous investigation.

You need
Mineral samples, mass balance, measuring cylinder.

What to do
- Carry out and record your measurements.
- Calculate the densities. Show your results in a table.
- Look at your results. Do they show that you identified the minerals in the previous investigations correctly?

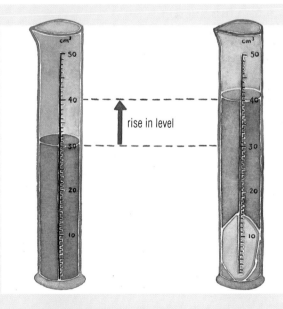

rise in level

Useful information
- The picture shows you how to measure the volume of a solid. Put the solid in water in a measuring cylinder and see how much the level rises on the scale.
- To calculate density divide the mass (in g) by the volume (in cm³).

F3.5 Looking at rocks

The rock in the photographs are sedimentary. They were made from fragments deposited at the bottom of an ancient sea hundred of millions of years ago. In time, more and more deposits settled above the fragments. Squashed together, the fragments slowly turned into layers of solid rock. Later, as the sea level changed, the rocks became exposed on land.

A Sandstone

B Limestone

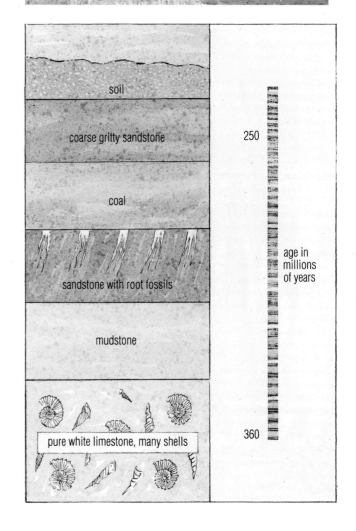

The particles in soil are mainly fragments from the rock underneath. The biggest fragments in the soil we call stones. Look at the photographs of the rocks and of the soil in the field.

1 Which of the two types of rock do you think is under the soil in the field? Explain your answer.

2 What made the surface of the rock break up so that soil was formed?

3 Where did the stones come from?

A time problem

Paul and Emma are looking at a chart showing layers of sedimentary rock in a cliff. Paul wants to know how there can be bits of shell in the limestone when it is on dry land. Emma would like to know why the youngest rock is at the top and the oldest at the bottom.

4 About how old is the oldest rock in the chart?

5 About how old is the youngest rock in the chart?

6 About how long ago was the coal formed?

7 How do you think cliffs might be formed?

8 How are sedimentary rocks formed?

9 What answer would you give Paul?

10 What answer would you give Emma?

soil

coarse gritty sandstone

coal

sandstone with root fossils

mudstone

pure white limestone, many shells

250

age in millions of years

360

Changed rocks

Sometimes, igneous and sedimentary rocks may be changed or 'baked' by great pressure or heat underground. This turns them into very different rocks from what they were before. Rocks changed in this way are called **metamorphic** rocks.

11 What is the metamorphic rock in the photograph used for?

12 Try to find out the names of some other metamorphic rocks.

13 Look up the word *metamorphose* in a dictionary. What does it mean?

Investigate
Fieldwork

To find out about the rocks, it is important to study them outside in the places they are found. You can see a page from a geologist's notebook in the diagram. With your group:

- List the things you think should be recorded during your fieldwork.
- Choose an area near you where rocks can be studied outside. It may be the school, a dry stone wall or a graveyard.
- List the things you need for your fieldwork.
- Ask your teacher to check your plans.
- Carry out the fieldwork and record your findings.
- Make a report of your findings.

Did you know?

Over millions of years, Earth movements can push layers of rock into **folds**. Sometimes, rocks can be folded so much that the oldest rock ends up on top. Whole mountain ranges can be formed from folded rock.

Marble: a metamorphic rock formed from limestone.

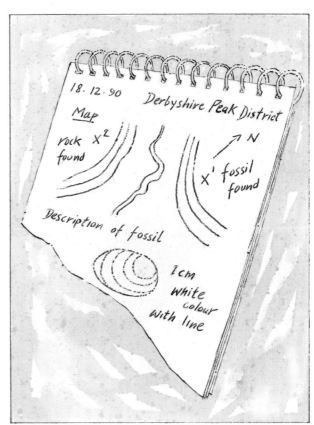

Local rock

Rocks have many uses. For example, stone-built houses are made from lumps of rock. This was a common method of building before bricks became popular.

14 Are there any stone-built houses in your area? If so, where?

15 In what other ways have rocks been used in your area?

16 What is the most common rock used in your area? Is it found locally? If so, where?

Stepping stones

Symbol mix-up

snow

hail

rain

temperature

wind direction

sunshine

20

showers with some sun

cloudy

The weather expert was going to give a lecture but someone accidently mixed up the symbols and labels she had made to show the audience.

1 See if you can sort out the mess by copying the symbols and writing the correct label with each one.

Water cycle

Dave heard someone say that water is never used up, it just goes round and round. Dave can't understand what this means.

2 How would you explain it to him?

Weather map

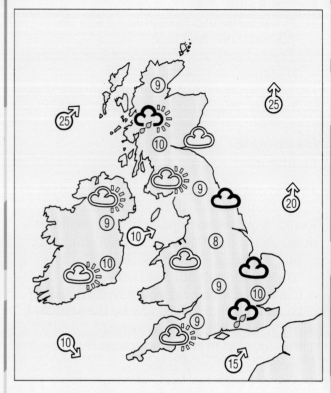

Here is a weather forecaster's map.

3 What is the weather like
in Cornwall?
in the North of Scotland?
in London?
in Wales?

Wind force

4 Estimate the Beaufort number of the wind blowing in the picture.

Legends

People have always tried to explain how earthquakes and volcanoes are caused. The Romans thought that the god of fire, Vulcan, lived inside volcanoes. The Greeks believed that Poseidon caused earthquakes by jumping up and down.

7 Invent your own legend to explain all of the things that happen during volcanoes and earthquakes. Make a poster to show the characters of your legend.

8 If you could travel back through time, how would you explain volcanoes and earthquakes to an Ancient Greek or Roman?

Crossword

5 Copy and complete the crossword.

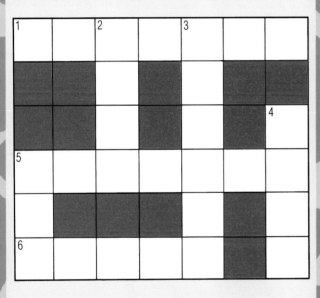

Across
1 Molten rock can flow from this.
5 A type of rock formed from molten material.
6 The layers in this rock make it useful for roofs.

Down
2 A flowing, molten material.
3 Not dormant.
4 This is needed to melt rocks.
5 This can make bubbles in rocks.

Rockword

6 Solve these clues. Use the first letter of each answer to make a word which is a type of sedimentary rock.

1 Useful for looking closely at rocks.
2 When water changes into this, it can split rocks.
3 Useful materials found in rocks.
4 Volcano in Sicily.
5 Rocks formed from fragments.
6 Carried from one place to another.
7 The ——— rocks are usually at the bottom.
8 Essential for fieldwork.
9 Process of wearing away.

Out of order

9 The following sentences should describe the rock cycle, but they are out of order: Put the sentences in the correct order.

A Sediment is buried as more deposits settle.
B Weathering weakens the rocks.
C Small fragments are carried out to sea.
D Compressed sediment eventually turns into hard rock.
E Rivers transport the fragments of rock.
F The weakened rock is eroded in fragments.
G Heavy fragments are deposited near the shore.
H Layers of sediment are deposited on the sea bed.

OXFORD
SCIENCE
programme

G   The Earth in space

G1.1 Sun, Earth and Moon

Sunrise

Sunset

The photographs above show the Sun rising and setting. In your group discuss the following questions. When you have agreed on your answers write them down. You may need to draw some diagrams to help you.

1. In what direction do you have to look to see the Sun rise in the morning?
2. In what direction do you have to look to see the Sun set in the evening?
3. Why does the Sun appear to move across the sky?
4. Which way does it move?
5. At what time of day does the Sun appear to be highest in the sky?
6. In which direction do you have to look to see the Sun at midday?
7. Does the sun follow the same path in summer and in winter?

The photographs below show a shadow at different times on a summer's day.

8. Which photograph was taken first? Explain your answer.
9. What happened to the shadow during the day? Why?
10. Could this idea be used to find out what time it is? If so how?
11. When each photograph was taken, would the shadow have looked the same if the Sun had been shining on a winter's day instead of a summer's day?
12. If you could move the pillar instantly to some other part of the world, would its shadow still be the same?
13. At the time each photograph was taken, would the time have been the same in other parts of the world?

Lighting-up time

Lighting-up time is the time that the street lights are turned on. It varies depending on the time of year and where you happen to be. Look at the lighting-up times shown in the table.

14 How do the lighting-up times change?

15 What month contains the day with the most daylight?

16 What month contains the day with the least daylight?

17 Why do you think the word 'approximate' has been used when giving the lighting-up time for each month?

18 Why do you think the length of daylight changes during the year?

19 On any particular day, do you think the number of hours of daylight in Britain, at the North Pole and on the Equator would be the same? Explain your answer.

Approximate lighting-up time	(p.m.)
January	4 : 30
February	5 : 30
March	6 : 30
April	8 : 30
May	9 : 00
June	9 : 30
July	9 : 00
August	8 : 30
September	7 : 00
October	5 : 30
November	4 : 00
December	4 : 00

Why do we get night and day?

You can use a simple model to help you find out the answer to the question above.

Investigate

■ Use a ball and a torch to investigate why we get night and day.

■ Explain how your model shows the difference between night and day?

You need
A large ball for the Earth, a torch for the Sun.

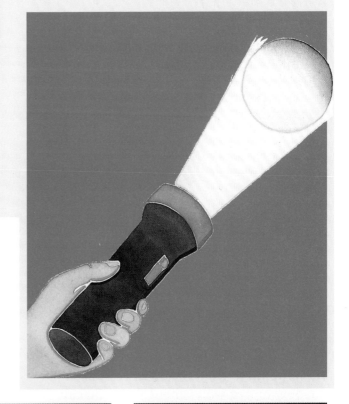

Looking at the Moon

The pictures of the Moon show how it appeared on two different dates. With your group:

20 Write down as many things as you can about the Moon.

21 Try to agree on the five most important.

22 Draw all of the shapes you think the Moon can make.

23 How long does it take for the Moon to make all of these shapes?

24 Does the Moon really change its shape?

25 Why do you think the Moon appears to change its shape?

26 Does the moon appear to move across the sky?

27 Is the moon visible on every clear night?

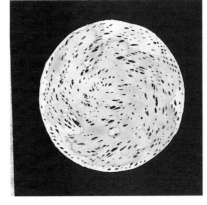

G1.2 What shape is the Earth?

The photograph of the Earth was taken from space. Darren says it shows that the Earth is a flat disc, the same shape as a coin. Sharon says that the Earth is round like a ball.

1 With your group, discuss what shape you think the Earth is.

2 In your group, talk about how you could find out what shape the Earth really is.

Ships and horizons

The person in the picture is watching a ship as it sails over the horizon.

3 What is the horizon?

4 What do the events in the pictures tell us about the shape of the Earth?

Eclipses

If you stand in front of a light you cast a shadow on the wall behind you. You can make different shadows with your hands. The Earth has a shadow behind it. If the Moon passes into this shadow we call it an **eclipse** of the Moon.

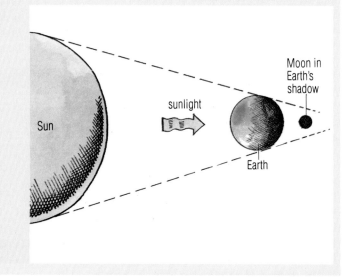

Investigate

■ Use a torch and two spheres to make a model showing an eclipse of the Moon.

■ Use different shaped objects to show how the shape of a shadow can be used to find out the shape of the Earth.

Images of Earth

Pictures of the Earth are used a lot on television, in advertisements and in other places. Sometimes the whole Earth is shown, sometimes just part.

5 Make a list of all the places where you have seen pictures of the Earth.

6 Which of these helped you to see the shape of the Earth?

7 Why do you think the picture was used in each case?

Many years ago, most people thought that the Earth was flat. Some people still do.

8 If you thought like this how would you try to convince someone that the Earth was flat?

A special planet

A science book describes the Earth as 'a large, spherical, self-contained planet'.

9 Explain in your own words what you think this means.

10 Why does this mean that we have to take great care of our planet?

11 In what ways are we not taking good care of the Earth?

12 Discuss your ideas with your group.

Changing ideas

In 700 BC, the Assyrian Empire fell. At its height, it had stretched for just 1400 miles from Egypt to Babylon. The Persian Empire which replaced it also stretched for no more than 1400 miles. At that time, the majority of people only saw a very small area of the Earth. They had no reason to think that the Earth was not flat.

Before the Ancient Greeks, everyone probably thought that the Earth was flat. In 500 BC the Greek Hecataeus of Miletus suggested that the Earth was a circular slab with a diameter of about 5000 miles. This seemed plenty large enough to hold all of the known world.

13 What is the furthest place that anyone in your group has heard of? How far away is it?

14 If the Earth was as Hecataeus suggested, what would its area be?

Here are two other questions about the Earth that worried people in ancient times:
What is holding the Earth up?
Does it extend down forever?

15 What do you think people meant by 'forever'?

In about 450 BC, the Greek philosopher Philolaus of Taventum put forward the idea that the Earth was a sphere. An untested idea like this is called a **hypothesis**.

16 How do you think Philolaus might have tested his hypothesis?

Moon watch

The different shapes that the Moon appears to make are called its **phases**. To study the phases, you need to observe the Moon over several months. Here is an investigation for the whole class.

Investigate

- Observe the phases of the Moon.
- Record your observations in charts like the one on the right.
- Work out what the shape must have been when you could not see the Moon.

Centuries ago, people developed their ideas about dates and calendars by watching the motion of the Sun and Moon.

1 See what you can find out about calendars and why years were divided into months.

20/3	21/3	22/3	23/3	24/3	25/3	26/3
27/3	28/3	29/3	30/3	31/3	1/4	2/4
3/4	4/4	5/4	6/4	7/4	8/4	9/4
10/4	11/4	12/4	13/4	14/4	15/4	16/4

Testing ideas

We can look at the surface of the moon without hurting our eyes.

2 Do we see the Moon because it gives off its own light? Or do we see it because it reflects light from the Sun? Discuss your ideas with your group. Draw a diagram to explain your answer.

3 Write down your ideas about why the Moon has different phases. Discuss these with your group.

Investigate

- Test your ideas about the Moon's shapes. Use a model to see if you can work out why the Moon has different phases.
- What did you discover? What explanation would you give to someone who wanted to know why the Moon has different phases.

You need
A large ball for the Earth, a small ball for the Moon, a torch for the Sun.

Moon talk

People sometimes refer to the Moon when writing or speaking.

4 In your group decide what you think the following expressions mean:
once in a blue moon
moonstruck
harvest moon

5 Try to think of some more expressions which use the word 'moon'.

6 There are lots of superstitions about the Moon. See how many you can find.

Testing a superstition

Here is one superstition about the Moon: if seeds are planted under a full Moon they will grow into healthier plants.

Investigate

■ Find out if this superstition is true. (If you prefer, you could test another superstition about the Moon instead.)

A closer look at the Moon

The picture on the right is a close-up photograph of the Moon. On the surface, you can see craters, mountains and 'seas'. These are not really seas at all. They are flat areas of land. But early observers thought they looked like seas. Answer these questions with your group:

7 How do you think the craters might have been formed on the Moon?

8 There are very few craters like this on the Earth. Why do you think this is so?

9 The surface of the Earth is continuously being changed but the surface of the Moon hardly changes at all. Why do you think there is a difference?

Moon landing

The first people to land on the Moon were two American astronauts, Neil Armstrong and Buzz Aldrin, in 1969. The photograph on the right was taken during their mission. They landed in a spacecraft which started its journey from Earth aboard a much larger, streamlined rocket.

10 The spacecraft in the photograph was more flimsy and less powerful than the rockets used on Earth. Why was this?

11 Can you tell anything about the Moon's atmosphere from clues in the photograph? Explain your answer.

12 On a later mission, a special car called a lunar buggy was used on the Moon. In what ways do you think a Moon car would be different from one used on Earth?

13 Find out what you can about the race to put people on the Moon.

You need

Diary or calendar which gives the dates of new Moons, seeds (like cress) which are quick and easy to grow, something to grow the seeds in.

Things to think about

How will you make sure that your test is fair?

G1.4 The seasons

The photographs were taken in Britain at four different times of the year.

1 What season is shown in each photograph?
2 How are the seasons different from each other?
3 If the photographs had been taken in Australia, what months might they show?
4 Why do we have seasons?

A yearly journey

The Earth moves around the Sun once every 365 days and spins on its axis, once every 24 hours. The axis is tipped over.

Investigate

Use a model of the diagram below to test out your ideas about the seasons.

You need
A ball as the Earth, a torch as the Sun.

What to do
- Use your model to show why we have day and night. Do all parts of the world have day and night at the same time?
- Use your model to show why some of our nights are shorter than others.

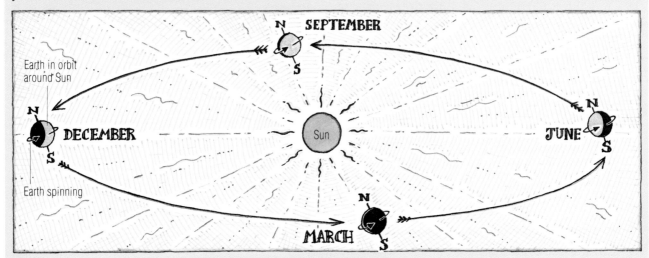

Earth in orbit around Sun

SEPTEMBER

DECEMBER

Sun

JUNE

Earth spinning

MARCH

A different angle

Here are two investigations which may help you understand the seasons.

Investigate

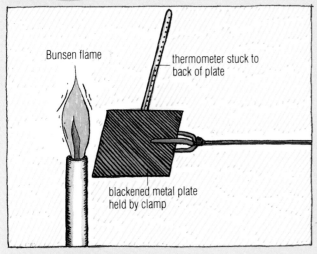

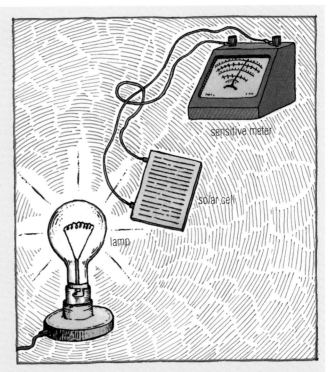

- Tip the plate. What happens to the temperature?
- Explain your observations.

- Tip the solar cell. What happens to the reading on the meter?
- Explain your observations.

High in the sky

Louise measures how the **altitude** and direction of the Sun changes on different dates. You can see her readings in the table.

5 What is special about the dates she has chosen?

6 What can you work out from her readings?

7 Draw graphs of the data for display.

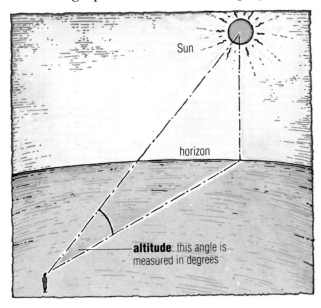

altitude: this angle is measured in degrees

Time	Altitude of Sun in degrees	Direction of Sun from north in degrees
Date: 21 March and 21 September		
7.30 a.m.	sunrise	90
9.00 a.m.	20	130
10.30 a.m.	30	160
12.00 noon	35	180
2.00 p.m.	30	220
3.30 p.m.	15	250
4.30 p.m.	sunset	270
Date: 21 June		
5.30 a.m.	sunrise	50
7.00 a.m.	20	80
9.30 a.m.	45	130
12.00 noon	50	180
4.00 p.m.	35	260
6.30 p.m.	sunset	310
Date: 21 December		
9.30 a.m.	sunrise	130
12.00 noon	13	180
2.30 p.m.	sunset	230

The Earth is just one of a whole family of planets that move round the Sun. The Sun and its planets are called the **Solar System**. Use the information about the planets in the table below to help you answer these questions:

1 What is meant by a *day*?
2 What is meant by a *year*?
3 Which is the largest planet?
4 Which is the smallest planet?
5 Which planets are warmer than Earth?
6 Which planets are colder than Earth?

7 Which planet spins most quickly?
8 Which planet spins most slowly?
9 Which planet moves around the Sun in the shortest time?
10 Which planet moves around the Sun in the longest time?
11 Earth is almost certainly the only planet in the Solar System with life on it. Why do you think this might be?
12 Use the information in the table and anything else you can find out to write descriptions of some of the planets.

Planet	Diameter in km	Distance from Sun in millions km	Time to spin once	Time to go around Sun once	Number of moons	Surface temp. in °C	Surface gravity x Earth's
Mercury	4876	58	59 days	88 days	0	350	0.4
Venus	12 104	108	243 days	225 days	0	480	0.9
Earth	12 756	150	24 hours	365 days	1	22	1.0
Mars	6787	228	24 hours	2 years	2	− 23	0.4
Jupiter	142 796	778	10 hours	12 years	16	− 150	2.3
Saturn	120 000	1425	10 hours	29 years	17	− 180	0.9
Uranus	50 800	2867	16 hours	84 years	15	− 210	0.8
Neptune	48 600	4486	19 hours	164 years	2	− 220	1.1
Pluto	4000	5900	6 days	248 years	1	− 230	0.1

Planets not shown to scale

Looking for patterns

If you study the data in the table on the opposite page, you may be able to see patterns. In other words, you may be able to see links between the way the numbers change in different columns.

13 What patterns can you find in this data?

14 Can you explain any of these patterns? If so, which ones.

15 Plot graphs to show these patterns.

Did you know?

Some of the gases in our atmosphere behave like the glass in a greenhouse. They trap the Sun's heat and warm the Earth. This is called the **greenhouse effect**. Carbon dioxide is our main greenhouse gas. There is much more carbon dioxide in Venus's atmosphere than Earth's and it is the greenhouse effect that makes Venus so hot.

Finding out about the planets

Unmanned spacecraft have reached Mercury, Venus and Mars, and travelled close to Jupiter, Saturn and Neptune. The longest missions have taken over ten years because of the huge distances covered.

16 Find out what you can about missions to the planets. Present your findings in an interesting and attractive way.

17 Why do you think that manned missions are so much more difficult than unmanned ones? How many reasons can you think of?

Imagine that your group has to plan a manned mission to another planet.

18 What would be the problems of sending a manned mission to Jupiter?

19 Which planet do you think would be the easiest to send a manned mission to? Give reasons for your choice?

G2.1 Thinking about gravity

Discuss the following with your group:

1. Why does the skier move *down* the slope?
2. What difference does it make if the slope is steeper?
3. What difference does it make if the slope is longer?
4. Why is it more difficult to ride a bicycle up a hill than down?
5. Why is it harder if the hill is steeper?
6. What happens to the speed of a diver during a dive?
7. In the picture below, which way does the brick fall when
    John in England drops it?
    Kiri in New Zealand drops it?
    Sumi on the Equator drops it?
8. What does this tell you about gravity?

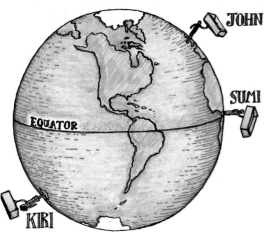

Dropping things

Investigate

Try dropping objects of different mass. Find out if they all fall in the same way.

You need
Paper, Plasticine, tube with water in it, stopwatch, thread, tissue paper.

What to do
- Drop a sheet of paper. Now screw the sheet of paper into a ball and drop it. Does this make any difference to the fall?
- Make different shapes from Plasticine. Drop these down a tube of water. Time how long each one takes. Is it the same for each?
- What answer would you give to someone who asks: 'Why do some things fall more quickly than others?'
- Discuss these questions with your group and write down your answers:
  When skydivers jump from an aeroplane do they get faster and faster as they fall? What happens when they open their parachute?
- Test your ideas using a model parachute and a Plasticine person.

Changing ideas

For centuries, people have puzzled over gravity. There are still many things which we do not understand about it. Try comparing your own ideas about gravity with the ideas developed by scientists over many centuries:

Aristotle (384-322 BC)

Aristotle's idea was that everything was made from four basic 'elements': earth, water, air and fire. Earth is heavy, fire is light and the others are in between. He thought that some things were heavier than others because they had different amounts of the elements in them. He said that light things naturally tend to move upwards, while heavy things tend to fall downwards. So the heavier something was, the faster it would fall.

Galileo Galilei (1564-1642)

Galileo wanted to disprove Aristotle's ideas, which had been used for centuries. He predicted that gravity would affect all falling objects in the same way. To try out his ideas, he dropped metal weights from a tower, probably in Pisa in Italy. He found that, when different masses were dropped at the same time, they hit the ground together. He realised that light things (like feathers) only fall slowly because they are more affected by air resistance.

Galileo may have used this tower for his gravity experiments.

Sir Isaac Newton (1642-1727)

Newton studied data about the motion of the planets collected over many years by astronomers. He used it to work out a mathematical way of explaining motion. In doing this, he developed many ideas about gravity that we still use today. Space scientists use his scientific laws to predict the motion of rockets and satellites.

A new, untested idea is called a **hypothesis**. In the descriptions of Aristotle, Galileo and Newton:

9 What examples can you find of someone putting forward a hypothesis?
10. What examples can you find of a hypothesis being tested?

Imagine that you have to give a talk explaining how our present ideas on how things fall are different from those of Aristotle.

11 What would you say in your talk?
12 See what else you can find out about Galileo and Newton.

Sir Isaac Newton (1642-1727)

When astronaut Alan Shepherd was on the Moon, he dropped a hammer and a feather at the same time. They both hit the surface together.

13 Why does this happen on the Moon but not on Earth?

G2.2 Up, down and around

Discuss these questions with your group and write down your answers:

1. Why is it more difficult to jump onto a step than jump off it?
2. Why is it difficult to jump very high?
3. What muscles do you use to jump?
4. How can you jump higher?
5. Why can some people jump higher than others?

Living on the Moon

Gravity on the Moon is only about one sixth of what it is on Earth. Discuss these questions with your group and write down your answers:

6. How much higher could you jump on the Moon?
7. How would the Moon's low gravity affect your weight?
8. How much more load could you carry on the Moon?
9. What difficulties would you have in walking on the Moon?
10. What effect would the Moon's low gravity have if you were trying to build a structure or a vehicle to use there?

It is unlikely that we will ever live on the Moon permanently. However, there are plans for building space observatories there. The Moon might also be used as a base for sending missions further into space.

11. What are observatories used for?
12. What are the advantages of building an observatory on the Moon rather than on the Earth?
13. What are the advantages of building a base for space missions on the Moon rather than on the Earth?
14. What problems would people have trying to live on the Moon? How could these be overcome?
15. Design your own Moon station. Draw a plan showing all the main equipment and facilities. It may help to read *Things to think about* on the right.

Things to think about
- What does a home have to provide you with on Earth?
- Why wouldn't an ordinary house be much good on the Moon?
- Have you listed all the things which people will need to keep alive on the Moon? Remember: there may not be a supply rocket for months or even years!
- What will happen to waste materials?

Uphill and down

Investigate

The pictures show some investigations you can carry out with a trolley.

You need
Runway supported so that you can change the height at one end, trolley, masses, metre rule, stopwatch, newtonmeters.

What to do
- Discuss the questions under each picture with your group.
- Carry out the investigations to test your answers.
- Present your results so that the rest of the class can see them. Use your ideas about gravity to explain your results.

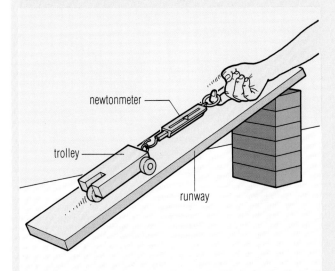

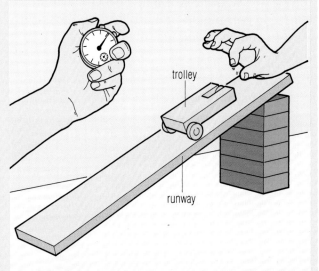

- How will the steepness of the slope affect the force needed to pull the trolley up the slope?
- How will the mass of the trolley affect the force needed?

- How will the steepness of the slope affect the time it takes for the trolley to run down the slope?
- How will the mass of the trolley affect the time taken?

Did you know?

All things have a force of attraction between them. Scientists call this the force of gravity. There is a gravitational pull between you and the person sat next to you but it is far too small to notice! However, the gravitational pull between you and the Earth is much stronger. And the pull between the Moon and the Earth is strong enough to hold the Moon in a circular orbit round the Earth.

Scientists do not know *why* there is gravity. But they have discovered several things about it. They know that more mass means a stronger gravitational pull. They also know that gravity gets weaker the further apart things are.

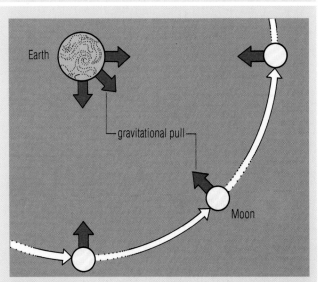

Gravitational force holds the Moon in orbit around the Earth.

G2.3 Further into space

Space has always fascinated people. Thousands of years ago, the Sun, Moon, planets and stars were being observed by people in China, Africa, India and the Arabic countries. From the early 1600s, observers were using telescopes. But the first person to actually go into space was the Russian Yuri Gagarin in 1961. He completed one orbit of the Earth on a flight which lasted just over one and a half hours.

Here are some important dates in the history of space exploration:

1042	Small, gunpowder rockets used in China
1942	First large rocket launched, in Germany
1957	First unmanned satellite: *Sputnik 1*, launched by the USSR
1961	First person in space: Yuri Gagarin (USSR)
1962	First 'fly-by' of a planet (Venus): *Mariner 2* (USA)
1964	First 'fly-by' of Mars: *Mariner 4*
1965	First spacewalk ('floating' outside a spacecraft)
1969	First people to land on the Moon: Neil Armstrong and Buzz Aldrin on the *Apollo 11* mission
1971	First spacecraft to orbit another planet (Mars): *Mariner 9*
1976	Two unmanned *Viking* spacecraft land on Mars
1977	*Voyager 2* launched on mission to 'fly-by' Jupiter, Saturn, Uranus and Neptune
1979	*Voyager 2* passes Jupiter
1981	*Voyager 2* passes Saturn
	First flight of space shuttle (USA)
1984	Space shuttle first used to recover a lost satellite
1986	*Voyager 2* passes Uranus
1989	*Voyager 2* passes Neptune

Launch of a space shuttle

Answer these questions with your group:
1. Why do you think it took humans so long to get into space?
2. Why are such large rockets needed to lift things into space?
3. With most rockets, only the top part completes the journey into space. The rest is cast off and wasted. Why do you think this is?
4. How long did it take *Voyager 2* to reach Neptune?
5. Why do you think it took so long?
6. What problems would there be in keeping a spacecraft working for such a long time?

Space mission

A spacecraft is launched into orbit around the Earth. It travels to another planet. When it arrives, it goes into orbit around that planet.
7. Describe the journey of the spacecraft, explaining how gravity affects each stage.

The Solar System and beyond

The Solar System is made up of the **Sun**, its **planets**, and the **moons** which orbit the planets. The Sun is a star. It only looks bigger and brighter than other stars because it is closer to us. Astronomers think that other stars probably have planets of their own.

The Sun is part of a huge collection of stars known as a **galaxy**. Our galaxy is called the **Milky Way**. It contains more than 100 billion stars. It is only one of billions of galaxies which make up the **Universe**.

Space distances

So far, no spacecraft has travelled beyond our Solar System. The distances are too vast. Look at the chart on the right. It shows the Sun and some of the planets with distances drawn to scale. On this scale, the nearest star (apart from the Sun) would be 800 metres away!

Scientists sometimes measure space distances in **light years**. A light year is the distance travelled by light in one year. And light travels at a speed of about 300 000 kilometres per *second*! The nearest star we can see (apart from the Sun) is *Alpha Centauri*. It is 4.3 light years away. When we look at it, we see it as it was 4.3 years ago!

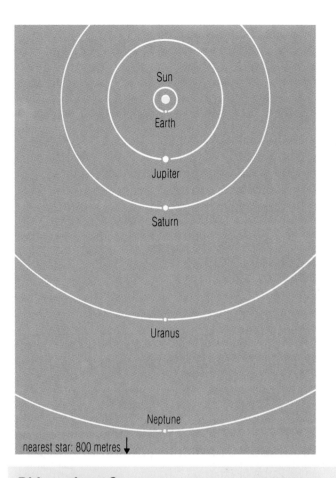

nearest star: 800 metres ↓

Answer these questions with your group:

8 Planets and stars just look like bright dots in the sky. What difference is there in the way they give out light?
9 Nick wants to know the difference between planets, stars and galaxies. What would you tell him?
10 Someone says that you are looking back in time when you look at the stars. What do they mean?
11 Nick wants to know why we can't send spacecraft to explore planets around other stars. What would you tell him?

Here are some difficult questions. You will need a calculator to work out the answers.

12 How far does light travel in one year?
13 How far is *Alpha Centauri* in kilometres?
14 If *Voyager 2* was travelling to *Alpha Centauri*, how long would it take?

Did you know?

The Andromeda Galaxy is a 'close' neighbour of our galaxy. It is only 2 million light years away'.

G3.1 Depending on the Sun

Our lives depend on the Sun.

1 List all of the things that we get from the Sun.

2 Write down your ideas about why there would be no life on Earth without the Sun.

3 Write down what you think would happen if the Sun suddenly stopped shining.

4 Discuss your ideas in your group.

5 Put all your ideas together in a single list.

6 Display this list for the rest of the class to see.

Energy from the Sun

A rabbit, grass and a fox are an example of a food chain.

7 What is a food chain?

8 Draw the food chain with a rabbit, grass and a fox in it.

9 Where do the rabbit and the fox get their energy from?

10 Where does the grass get its energy from?

The Sun is useful to us in many ways. Some are direct, such as providing warmth. Others are less direct, such as helping to grow the trees millions of years ago that ended up as coal. You may be able to find some examples in the picture. With your group:

11 List the different ways that the Sun is (or has been) useful to us.

Healthy houseplants

Plants need the right conditions to grow properly.

12 List all the things which you think plants need to grow.

Investigate

- Look at the advice labels from a range of houseplants.
- Make a chart to show the information you have found. It could look like this:

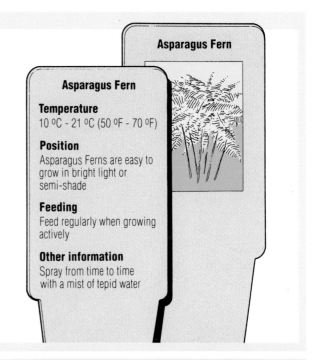

Name of plant	Watering instructions	Position	Temperature

- What things are common to all the labels?
- What things are needed to keep house-plants healthy throughout the year?

A gardener's problem

A friend is about to take up gardening as a hobby. She asks you several questions:

'How do plants grow?'
'What do plants need to grow?'
'Do plants need food to grow?'
'If so, how do they get their food?'

13 Discuss these questions in your group. When you have some answers, make a poster to display your ideas.

Investigate

Test an idea from your list. You could share out the ideas amongst your group.

What to do

- Plan how you will test your idea. Make sure that your plan covers the points on the right.
- Carry out your tests.
- Write a report for your friend describing what you found out.

Asparagus Fern

Asparagus Fern

Temperature
10 °C - 21 °C (50 °F - 70 °F)

Position
Asparagus Ferns are easy to grow in bright light or semi-shade

Feeding
Feed regularly when growing actively

Other information
Spray from time to time with a mist of tepid water

Things to think about
- What idea are you going to test?
- What equipment will you need?
- How are you going to carry out your test?
- How will you make sure that you are only testing one idea at a time?
- What are you looking for?
- How will you record and present your results?

G3.2 Food for plants

This is how scientists think that plants live and grow:

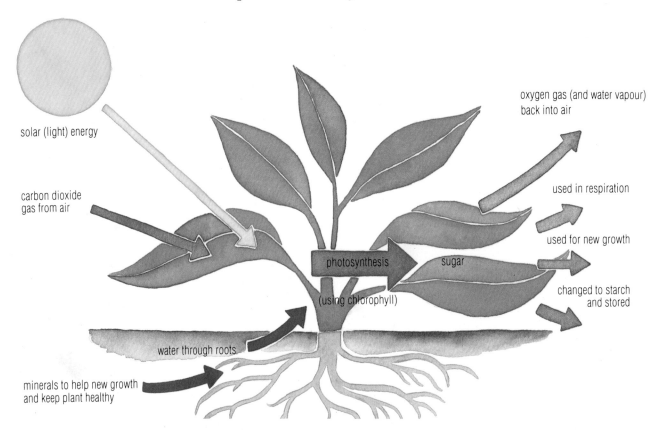

All living things need food to live and grow. Animals have to find their food. Plants make their own. They take in simple substances like water from the soil and carbon dioxide gas from the air. They use the energy in sunlight to turn these into food such as sugar. Scientists call this **photosynthesis**. Plants have a green chemical in their leaves to absorb the Sun's energy. This chemical is called **chlorophyll**. It gives leaves their green colour. When plants make food, they store it in their leaves and roots to be used later. Like other animals, we cannot make food. But we can eat plants and use their food.

During photosynthesis, plants make oxygen as well as food. They need some of this oxygen. But the rest comes out of their leaves and into the atmosphere.

Living things use oxygen to get energy from their food. This process is called **respiration**. When animals respire, they make carbon dioxide which they breathe out. Plants also respire and make carbon dioxide. But, for photosynthesis, they have to take in extra carbon dioxide through their leaves.

Below, is another way of showing what happens during photosynthesis:

carbon dioxide + water $\xrightarrow[\text{using chorophyll}]{\text{light energy}}$ **oxygen + sugar** ⋯⋯ ↗ **some used in respiration**
→ **some changed and used (with minerals) to make new plant material**
↘ **some changed and stored as food (starch)**

Here are three words: *respiration*, *chlorophyll*, *photosynthesis*.
1 Which of them means 'making food by using the energy in sunlight'?
2 Which of them means 'getting energy from food'?

Answer these questions about the scientists' ideas on the opposite page:
3 How do plants get their food?
4 Why do plants need light?
5 What gas do plants need for photosynthesis?
6 What gas do plants make during photosynthesis?
7 Why do animals eat plants?
8 Why do animals and plants need oxygen?
9 What gas is made during respiration?

Look at the picture on the right.
10 Why do the plants have green leaves?
11 What do you think is stored in the bulging parts at the bottom of the plants?

Comparing and testing

You have discussed your own ideas about the things plants need to live and grow. You have also seen the scientists' ideas.
12 How do the scientists' ideas compare with your own? Make a table to show the similarities and differences:

How my ideas are the <u>same</u> as the scientists' ideas	How my ideas are <u>different</u> from the scientists' ideas

Investigate

- In your group make a list of the ideas that could be tested.
- Choose one of these ideas. Plan an investigation to test it.
- Carry out your investigation.

Depending on plants

Green plants are essential for all life on Earth. Only plants can use the energy in sunlight to make food. Animals eat plants, or they eat meat from animals which have fed on plants. So, through food chains, plants provide the energy for all living things.

Plants are also vital for keeping the atmosphere in balance. Animals use up oxygen and make carbon dioxide. But plants take carbon dioxide out of the atmosphere and make oxygen.

13 Dave can't understand why, if we are breathing in oxygen all the time, it never gets used up. How would you explain it?
14 Large areas of the world's forests are being cut down. What would happen to the atmosphere if most of the Earth's plants were destroyed?
15 Carbon dioxide is also made by burning fossil fuels like gas, coal and oil (and the petrol which comes from it). What would happen to the atmosphere if we started burning a lot more of these fuels?

G3.3 Investigating photosynthesis

Here are four investigations for you to do. You can use them to test the scientists' ideas about photosynthesis.

Investigate

- Read through the investigations. Make a list of the equipment you need for each one.
- Carry out your investigations.
- Discuss your results. Do they support the scientists' ideas about photosynthesis?

Gas in . . .

Find out what gas from the air is used in photosynthesis.

Useful information
- You can use hydrogencarbonate indicator to test for carbon dioxide in air. The indicator is red/purple if there is no carbon dioxide. It turns red and then yellow if enough carbon dioxide is present.
- The picture shows you how to set up the experiment.
  Why are three tubes needed?

What to do
- Set up your experiment.
- Leave the tubes for about 12 hours.
  What colour does the indicator turn in each one?
- What did you find out from your results?

Gas out . . .

Find out what gas is produced during photosynthesis.

Useful information
- The picture shows you how to collect gas from pond weed.
- The plant needs to be near a lamp for two or three days. Make sure that the lamp isn't too close or it will heat up the water.
- You should also set up a second experiment with pond weed in darkness. Why?
- Oxygen makes a glowing splint burn fiercely.
- Carbon dioxide turns lime water milky.

What to do
- Carry out your investigation.
- Test the gas collected.
- What did you find out from your results?

Testing for sugar

Test some leaves to find out whether they have sugar in them.

What to do
- Take some leaves from a plant which has been kept in the light for several days.
- Crush the leaves and test them with a sugar testing strip.
- Repeat this with leaves from a plant that has been kept in the dark for several days.
- What did you find out from your results?

sugar testing strip turns blue if sugar is present

crushed leaves (with a little water)

Chlorophyll and starch

Find out if a leaf needs chlorophyll in it in order to make starch.

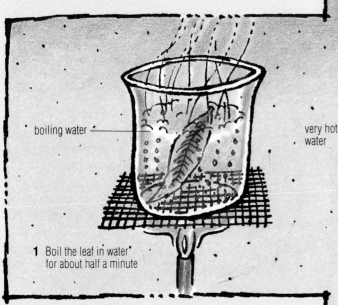

boiling water

1 Boil the leaf in water for about half a minute

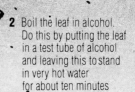
alcohol

very hot water

2 Boil the leaf in alcohol. Do this by putting the leaf in a test tube of alcohol and leaving this to stand in very hot water for about ten minutes

3 Soften the leaf by dipping it in boiling water again

Useful information
- If a leaf is **variegated**, it has different colours. Which parts have chlorophyll in?
- You can use iodine solution to test for starch. If starch is present, iodine solution changes from dark orange to dark blue.

What to do
- Take a fresh, variegated leaf and draw its outline. Mark on the parts that are green.
- Prepare and test the leaf as in the pictures. (Preparing the leaf as shown softens it, removes the chlorophyll and makes the results of your test easier to see).
- On your outline, mark on the parts of the leaf which contain starch.
- What did you find out from your results?

4 Test for starch by dropping iodine solution onto the leaf

iodine solution

Safety note: alcohol is highly inflammable. It must be kept away from flames.

G3.4 The best from your plants

Best value

Garden centres sell lots of different 'plant foods'. People buy them to make their plants healthier.

1 Look at some labels to find out what 'plant foods' are meant to do.

2 Are they really plant foods? What part do they play in making healthy plants?

Investigate

- Plan an investigation to find out which 'plant food' gives the best value for money.
- Discuss your plan with your teacher.
- Carry out your investigation and report on your findings.

Growing in a greenhouse

With a greenhouse, you can control the conditions in which plants grow.

3 List all of the things plants need for healthy growth.

4 List the conditions that could be controlled in a greenhouse.

Investigate

Use a model greenhouse (or a real one) to investigate the best conditions for growing plants.

You need
Seedlings, soil or compost, containers, materials for making a model greenhouse, items chosen by you.

What to do
- Discuss and plan your investigation with your group.
- Make a list of the things you need.
- Discuss your plan with your teacher.
- Carry out your investigation.
- Write a report on your investigation. Remember to describe the growing conditions, how you controlled them, and what you found out.

Things to think about
- What plants will you grow?
- How will you change the conditions in which they grow?
- Will your tests be fair?

Did you know?

Hydroponics is a way of growing plants without soil or any other solid growing material. The plant roots are kept in water which contains all the minerals they need. The minerals, temperature, light level and humidity can be monitored and controlled by a computer.

5 What are the advantages of a system like this?

6 What are the disadvantages?

Energy from grass

Sally keeps cattle on her farm. She is interested in finding out how much food energy is stored in grass. She wants to check whether her cows are getting enough food energy from her fields.

Investigate

Find out how much energy can be obtained from a beakerful of grass.

You need
Grass, items chosen by you.

Useful information
• We sometimes say that we are 'burning up' our food when we get energy from it. However, this happens in our bodies without any flames.
• Energy is measured in **joules.** 1000 joules is enough energy to heat 250 grams of water by 1°C.

Things to think about
• How can you release the energy from the grass?
• Does the grass need to be dried first?
• What form will this energy be in?
• How will you measure the energy released?
• Should you weigh the grass so that Sally knows how much of it you used?

What to do
▓ Plan your investigation.
▓ Ask your teacher to check your plan.
▓ Carry out your investigation.
▓ Write a letter to Sally telling her what you have found out.

Hydroponically grown plants

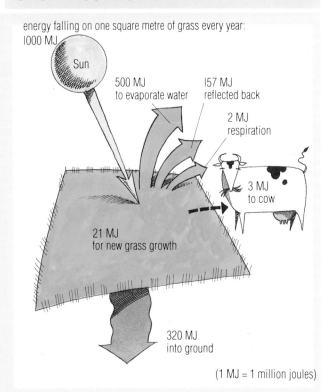

energy falling on one square metre of grass every year: 1000 MJ

Sun

500 MJ to evaporate water

157 MJ reflected back

2 MJ respiration

3 MJ to cow

21 MJ for new grass growth

320 MJ into ground

(1 MJ = 1 million joules)

In the diagram above, a patch of grass is receiving energy from the Sun. MJ stands for megajoule (million joules). Of the original 1000 MJ:

7 what percentage is used to grow new grass?

8 what percentage does the cow get by eating the grass?

G3.5 Energy from the Sun

Plants need the Sun's energy to grow. Through food chains, plants provide the energy for animals. So all living things get their energy from the Sun. But we don't only need energy from food. We need energy to run our homes, factories and transport as well.

The picture below shows our main sources of energy.

1 In your group, discuss the picture and make a list of the energy sources it shows.

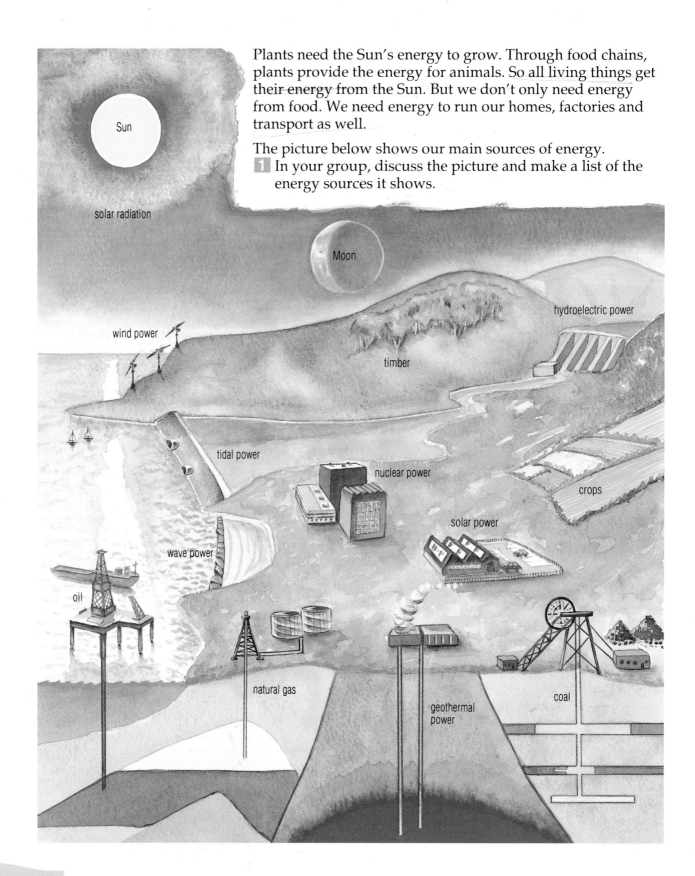

Sun

solar radiation

Moon

hydroelectric power

wind power

timber

tidal power

nuclear power

crops

wave power

solar power

oil

natural gas

geothermal power

coal

Starting with the Sun

Many of the energy sources in the picture on the opposite page got their energy from the Sun. Answer the following with your group. You might have to do some research first. The *Things to think about* underneath may start you off.

2 Find out how coal, oil and natural gas were formed.

3 Explain why coal, oil and natural gas are storing energy which originally came from the Sun.

4 Which of the other energy sources in the picture got their energy from the Sun. How did they get this energy?

Things to think about
- Coal, oil and natural gas were formed from the remains of animals and plants which lived millions of years ago.
- The Earth's winds are partly caused by hot air which rises over the equator.
- Tides are caused by the gravitational pulls of the Moon and the Sun.
- Water which evaporates from the sea eventually falls as rain.

Did you know?

In Edmonton, North London, there is a power station which uses household rubbish as its fuel. It burns 400 000 tonnes of it every year.

Biofuels

Wood is a fuel. It can be burnt to give heat. Alcohol is a fuel. Some cars run on alcohol made from sugar cane. Methane is a fuel. Rotting rubbish is one source of this gas. Fuels like this, which are made directly from plant or animal materials are called **biofuels**. All plant and animal materials, living or dead, are called **biomass**.

The chart below shows how biofuels can provide energy.

5 What are the advantages of using waste materials as a source of energy?

6 Some waste materials are not suitable for fuels. What examples can you think of? Why are they not suitable?

7 What might be some of the problems of growing more crops for fuel?

Plant material

Rotting rubbish

biofuel → burnt as fuel

biofuel → fermented to make alcohol which can be used as a fuel

biofuel → decomposed by bacteria to make methane gas, which is a fuel

Stepping stones

Moving Earth

Paul has just become interested in the Earth in space. He thinks that the reason we have day, night and seasons has something to do with the motion of the Earth. But he is not clear about how this works.

1 Draw a diagram and make some notes to help him.

Moon view

People call one of these a 'full Moon' and the other a 'new Moon'.

2 Which one do you think is which?

3 Why do they have these names?

Rachel has seen the dates of the full Moons (and new Moons) in her diary. She wants to know why they happen regularly, about every 28 days.

4 How would you explain this to her?

Sorting out space

planet
moon   Universe
star   galaxy
Solar System   sun

Tim has written these down. He is confused about the difference between them.

5 Design a chart or poster which will make it clear to him. Set out your chart or poster so that it shows the order of size.

Gravity model

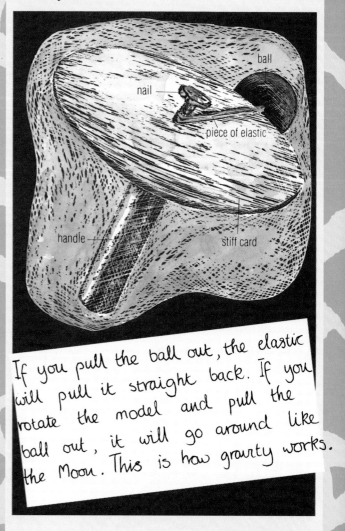

If you pull the ball out, the elastic will pull it straight back. If you rotate the model and pull the ball out, it will go around like the Moon. This is how gravity works.

You can see a student's ideas for a gravity model above.

6 Do you think this is a good model of gravity? Explain your answer. Mention any ways in which you think the model could be improved.

Flat Earth drama

One group of people thinks that the Earth is flat. Another group is trying to convince them that it is a sphere.

7 Write a short play about an argument between the two groups.

Sources of energy

Look at the sources of energy listed on the right.

8 Make a poster giving more information about each source. Show which of the sources supply energy which can be traced back to the Sun.

coal	wave
peat	solar
biomass	geothermal
oil	hydroelectric
natural gas	tidal
wind	nuclear

The Horticultural Society

As an expert on plants, you have been asked by your local Horticultural Society to give a talk. It will be called: 'Photosynthesis explained. How to grow healthy plants'.

9 Discuss and plan this talk with your group. You may be able to give the talk to the rest of your class, or make a tape of it. Instead of a talk, perhaps you could make a display for the Society to use at its next annual show.

Plant problems

Below, you can see some students' ideas about how plants get their food. You may not agree with them!

10 Write down what the students might have said if they had understood how plants get their food.

Writing the wrongs

When you start planning your garden, all the needs of the plants must be taken into account. These are food, water, light and warmth. Check the soil to see if it is acid or alkaline. Also check what fertilizer is needed. Fertilizer is the food that is the basic requirement for plants.

This extract has been taken from a gardening book. You may not be happy with the writer's understanding of science.

11 Write a letter to the author explaining what you think is correct and what is wrong.

OXFORD
SCIENCE
programme

H   The Earth in balance

H1.1 Looking at the environment

We use the word **environment** to describe our surroundings or the conditions in which we live. Here are some of the ways in which the word is used in books and newspapers:

> 'an urban environment'
> 'a rural environment'
> 'a domestic environment'
> 'a natural environment'
> 'a hostile environment'

1 What do you think they mean? Try to think of an example of each one.

Human beings share the planet Earth with thousands of other kinds of living things. For all these life forms to survive, it is essential that we take great care of our shared environment.

Look at the pictures. They show local environments in different parts of the world. For each scene:

2 Write down a word or phrase to describe the environment shown.

3 Suggest some of the living things that might inhabit the area.

In the pictures, you may also be able to see ways in which human activity has affected the natural environment. For each scene:

4 Describe the ways in which the natural environment is being used by people.

5 Explain how this human activity affects other living things in the environment.

6 Explain whether you think that this activity will cause any serious harm to the environment or its inhabitants.

We don't need to travel widely to have an effect on other environments. We often use machines, food, clothing and furniture which depend on materials found in other parts of the world.

7 Look again at the photographs. Use some of the scenes to explain how the behaviour of someone in one part of the world can affect the environment of people in other parts.

A

B

C

D

North America

B

Russia

Europe

D

A

Asia

Africa

E

South America

C

Australia

E

Litter is a serious problem in Britain today Not only is it unsightly. It can be extremely dangerous. Two major tragedies in the 1980s, the Bradford City Football Club fire and the King's Cross underground station fire were both started by litter catching alight.

In your groups:

1 Discuss your views about litter. List all the reasons why you think litter is a problem.
2 Select one local place which you think needs cleaning up.
3 Discuss ways in which the users of the place could be encouraged to be more tidy.
4 Decide on an action plan for reducing the litter problem.
5 Show your action plan to your teacher.
6 If you decide to carry out your action plan, keep an account of what you do. If possible, take photographs or make sketches to illustrate your account.

Playing surface

Look at the picture of the tennis match.

7 Describe how the grass looks in the different parts of the court.
8 Explain why the grass is in good condition in some parts but poor in others.
9 Make a list of the different kinds of all-weather sports surfaces which can be used instead of grass.
10 Describe the main advantages and disadvantages of these alternatives to grass.

Did you know?

Playing fields are seeded with specially selected blends of grasses to help them withstand the regular pounding from boots and training shoes. But even this turf can be damaged by over-use, particularly in cold and wet weather. This is why your school may ban you from walking across the school field when it is wet.

Firefighters at the scene of the King's Cross fire.

Damaged by leisure

Millions of people like to spend their leisure time outdoors. As a result, many natural environments are being damaged by over-use. Once vegetation has been trampled on and destroyed, wind and water can wear away the ground underneath.

About 9% of Britain's coastline is made up of sand dunes. Dunes are important because they support wildlife and act as a defence against the sea.

11 List the ways in which dunes might be damaged or destroyed by
   a natural causes **b** human activities.

Look at the photograph of the dune restoration work.

12 What method is being used to trap the sand and recreate the dune area?

13 Why should people stay away from the dunes until they are re-established?

Dune restoration

Planning problem

The picture shows a little-used path along the sides of a lake. The lake is filled by a series of small streams from nearby hills. The topsoil in the surrounding area is thin and the vegetation sparse. The landowners want to turn the lake into a watersports area with facilities for sailing and windsurfing.

14 With your group, list the possible effects on the environment of setting up a watersports area.

15 If you were granting planning permission for the watersports centre, what environmental conditions would you set? Give reasons for your decisions.

H1.3 A problem with waste

In Britain, we produce about 80 million tonnes of household, commercial and industrial waste every year. About 10% of this is burnt. The rest is taken to rubbish tips like old quarries. These are called **landfill** sites. They are becoming more and more difficult to find. Once sites near towns are full, new ones must be found. Often this means extra expense because of increased transport costs.

1 What are landfill sites?

2 About how many tonnes of waste are burnt in Britain every year?

Shops and offices often have large amounts of waste to get rid of.

3 What different types of waste are produced by shops and offices?

4 How could shops and offices reduce the amount of waste which they produce?

Rubbish survey

Investigate

Find out how much rubbish your family produces in a week.

Things to think about
- How will you record the items of rubbish produced by your family in a week?
- Would it be useful to know what proportion of the rubbish is paper, glass, metal, food scraps and plastics?
- Should you include rubbish which is disposed of away from home? For example: bus tickets, sweet wrappers, drinks cans.
- You should not handle dirty rubbish!

What to do
- Plan and carry out your survey. If your family already separates some rubbish for recycling, make a note of the details.
- Set out your findings in a clear way.
- Compare your findings with your group. Discuss how you could reduce the quantities of waste you produce.
- Design a poster to summarise your findings and your recommendations.

Landfill site

Recycling makes sense!

The Earth's raw materials are being used up at an ever increasing rate. One way of slowing the rate is to re-use things. This is called **recycling**. Paper, glass and aluminum are just some of the items of household waste which can be recycled easily.

5 What are *raw materials*? Give some examples.

It takes energy to make useful things out of raw materials. You can see some examples in the chart on the right. In Britain, most of this energy comes from power stations which burn fuels like coal and oil. Re-using materials helps to save energy. It is another reason why recycling makes sense.

6 There is a pint of milk on your doorstep. Make a list of all the way in which energy was used to get it there.

7 With your group, discuss and list the advantages and disadvantages of selling milk in glass bottles, plastic containers or waxed cardboard cartons.

8 Look again at your list of weekly rubbish. Make a note of the different items which could be kept separate for recycling.

9 Find out where your nearest glass, aluminium and paper banks are.

10 Make a display to explain to other people how we can save energy and help the environment by recycling materials.

Shopping survey

Customers in shops and supermarkets use millions of carrier bags every week. If people used heavy-duty shopping bags, or re-used carrier bags, natural resources would be used up less quickly. Our shopping bills might even be a little lower!

11 Plan a survey to find out how people carry their shopping home. Find out whether shopping habits vary with age or with the type of transport which people use when they go shopping.

12 Use the results of your survey to plan a campaign. With your group. The aim of the campaign should be to encourage shoppers and shopkeepers to reduce the use of carrier bags.

It takes more energy to make the car than a village in an underdeveloped country uses in a year.

Did you know?

About one tenth of our shopping bills is now spent on packaging. Most of this packaging goes in the dustbin.

H1.4 To keep or to quarry?

Natural resources such as coal, limestone, clay, sand and gravel are mined and quarried throughout the country. They provide materials for a wide range of industries. We need these materials. But to obtain them, the landscape is being changed for ever.

Limestone from the Mendips

Planners in Somerset have a problem. On the one hand, industry needs large amounts of limestone. On the other hand, removing the limestone causes environmental damage. Look at the photograph on the right. It shows a limestone quarry.

1 What might the area have looked like if the quarry had not been set up?

2 How has the environment been changed by the quarry?

3 Setting up a quarry doesn't only change the landscape. What other effects will quarrying have on the local area and the people who live there?

People have different opinions about whether quarrying on the Mendips should be allowed.

4 Read the opinions of the local people on the right. Then read the opinions and the information on the opposite page.

5 With your group, discuss what you have read and list the main points for and against quarrying.

6 Decide whether you think that limestone from the Mendips should be quarried and, if so, on what scale.

7 Explain your decision. You might find it helpful to use extracts from what you have read.

Local people

National industry

The building industry is the biggest customer for limestone. Much of it goes into the manufacture of cement. Limestone is also an essential material for the following industries: steel, plastics, drugs, glass and paper making.

Limestone chippings are used in Tarmac road surfaces, concrete, and as a base for laying railway tracks.

Chippings in use

Commercial interests

At present, quarries remove around 12 million tonnes of limestone from the Mendips each year. Its value is approximately £45 million.

The Mendips are an important source of drinking water. Reservoirs in the area provide water for around 600,000 people in Somerset and Avon. Extensive quarrying reduces the water-holding capacity. It also causes pollution. To provide the 600,000 people with alternative water would cost around £12 million per year.

Visitors to the area support businesses such as hotels, cafes, and show caves like the ones at Cheddar and Wookey Hole. Tourism employs far more people than quarrying, which is highly mechanised.

Tourists and other visitors

Cheddar

H1.5 Local conservation

Nature **conservation** means 'looking after the natural environment'. At one time, people's idea of conservation was looking after the countryside or setting up special nature reserves. Nowadays, more and more people want to bring 'nature' into towns.

In twenty years time, this estate may look more like . . .

this one . . .

The map on the opposite page shows a plan of a village on the outskirts of a busy town. The local councillors have considered various plans for development. These are the points which they think are most important:

- Housing is needed for an additional 25 families.
- New premises are needed for the health centre.
- There are occasional functions in the village hall. But local children and young people have no specially designed meeting places or play area.
- The river banks are overgrown and unsafe in places.
- When the last housing area was developed 15 years ago, many mature trees were felled. Since then, Dutch elm disease has killed more trees. Apart from in a few gardens, no trees have been planted in recent years.

With your group:
1. Study the map of the village carefully.
2. Discuss the needs of the villagers.
3. Decide on the best site or sites for the new housing. Explain your reasons carefully.
4. Draw a simplified map of the village. Show your choice of housing sites on it.
5. Show on your map where you would place containers to collect waste paper, empty cans and bottles for recycling.
6. Explain how you would use the rest of the land available to meet the needs of the villagers.
   Add extra details to your map to illustrate your answer.
7. Describe the recommendations you would make to improve the natural environment in and around the village.
8. If possible, make a model of the village which shows your ideas for the improvements.

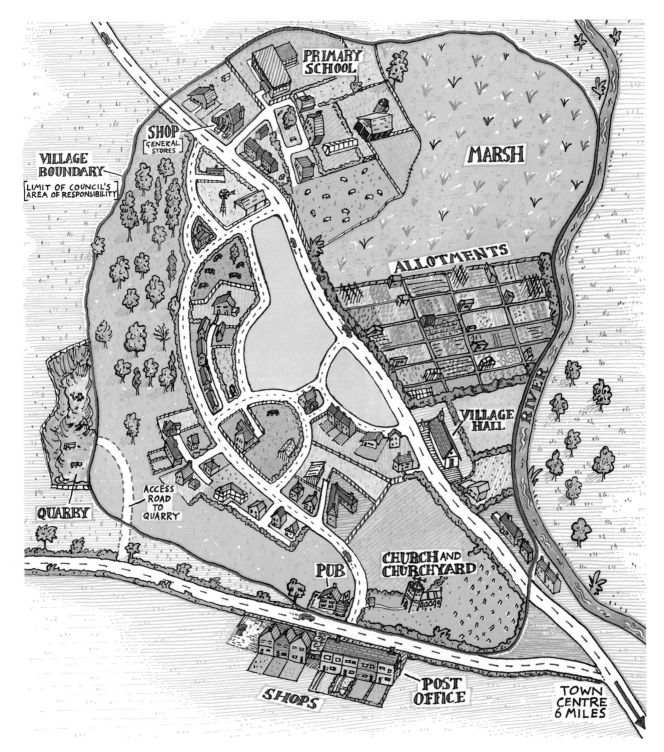

The village you have just discussed is on the edge of a busy town. If it was near the centre, there would be extra difficulties for families living there. For example, there might be:
- increased traffic
- office workers and shoppers using the streets for parking
- developers wanting to take over sites to build shops or offices.

Answer these:
9 With your group, discuss the extra needs of families who live near the centre of a town rather than on the edge. Make a list of your ideas.
10 Describe the extra difficulties the families in a town centre would face if they want to improve their environment.
11 Compare your ideas with other groups.

Fuels store energy.

1. List all the fuels you can think of. The pictures above may give you some ideas.
2. For each fuel in your list, decide whether it can be found naturally or whether it is made by processing natural materials.
3. Group the fuels according to how they are used. For example: in homes, factories, power stations.

The carbon cycle

Carbon is an important chemical for life on Earth. It can combine with other chemicals to make many different substances including carbon dioxide gas and the materials which plants and animals are made from.

The diagram on the opposite page shows how carbon can get used over and over again. It is an example of the **carbon cycle**.

Plants take in carbon dioxide gas from the air. They use the Sun's energy to combine this with water and minerals to make new plant material. This process is called **photosynthesis**. We eat plants as food, so our bodies have carbon in them. We get energy by 'burning up' our food, but without any flames! This is called **respiration**. When we respire, we make carbon dioxide gas which we breathe into the atmosphere.

90% carbon

20% carbon

Did you know?

Coal, oil and natural gas are called **fossil fuels**. Coal was formed from the rotting remains of trees and ferns which existed in swamps millions of years ago. The plants were trapped and crushed under layers of sediment which later hardened to form rock. Oil and natural gas were formed from the remains of microscopic animals and plants which lived in the sea millions of years ago. Today, oil companies search for layers of solid rock which may have oil and gas trapped in spongy rock beneath them.

carbon dioxide in air

plants

power stations

factories

vehicles

animals

microbes in soil

coal, natural gas and oil underground

The diagram isn't complete. The carbon cycle isn't just one, simple loop!

4 Copy your own version of the diagram onto the middle of a big sheet of paper.

5 Decide on the best places to put the following labels:

photosynthesis
respiration
food eaten

6 Use the information below to help you add more arrows and labels to your diagram. It might help to do these in pencil in case you need to rub them out.

Information

- Microbes in the soil feed on dead animals and plants.
- Microbes respire and give out carbon dioxide.
- Some animals eat meat as their food.
- Coal, natural gas and oil (including petrol) were formed from the remains of plants and microscopic animals which died millions of years ago.
- Burning fuels give out carbon dioxide.

Burning fossil fuels

When fossil fuels are burnt, energy is released as heat. Also released are carbon dioxide, water, and chemicals which have been 'locked up' in the fuels for up to 300 million years. Industrialised countries are burning fossil fuels at such a rate that the environment is being damaged.

7 List all the ways in which carbon dioxide is put into the atmosphere.

8 List all the ways in which carbon dioxide is taken out of the atmosphere.

9 The amount of carbon dioxide in the atmosphere is not remaining steady. It is slowly increasing. Why do you think this is?

10 Make a list of substances which pollute the atmosphere. Explain where you think each one comes from.

11 Not all energy sources take part in the carbon cycle. How many of these **alternative energy** sources do you know? Make a list, with a simple explanation of how we can get useful energy from each.

Microbes are tiny organisms (living things) which can only be seen under a microscope. They can be found on plants, animals, food and even floating around in the air.

Rot or not

If you leave grass cuttings, they will eventually decompose (rot away). This is because microbes feed on them and change them into a brown liquid. Materials like grass, which decompose because microbes feed on them, are called **biodegradable** materials.

1. Make a list of substances which you think are biodegradable.
2. Make a list of substances which you think are *not* biodegradable.

Gases from microbes

Gardeners often put garden rubbish and food scraps on a compost heap. Oxygen-loving microbes in the compost heap gradually change these biodegradable materials into useful fertilizer. As the materials decompose, the microbes produce carbon dioxide gas. They also release energy in the form of heat.

Some microbes can survive in places where there is no oxygen. Peat bogs, stagnant pools, swamps and paddy fields all contain microbes like this. These oxygen-hating microbes do not produce carbon dioxide when they feed. Instead, they produce methane gas. This is the same gas as the natural gas found with oil.

Did you know?

There are oxygen-hating microbes in the guts of many animals (including humans). They make 'wind' which builds up in the gut and has to be released.

There are 1300 million cows in the world. Together, they release about 100 million tonnes of methane gas into the atmosphere every year!

3. Victorian gardeners would sometimes put a thick layer of rotting compost under their topsoil so that they could enjoy early crops of strawberries and peas. Why would it have this effect?
4. What gas is produced by oxygen-loving microbes?
5. What gas is produced by oxygen-hating microbes?

Making a biogas generator

Methane gas is a useful fuel. It can be made in special gas generators where microbes digest animal droppings, seaweed or any material which will rot. Gas made by microbes is sometimes called **biogas**.

Investigate

Make a biogas generator like the one in the diagram.

You need
Grass cuttings or other biodegradable material, items shown in the diagram.

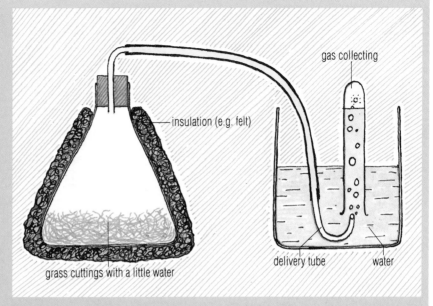

gas collecting

insulation (e.g. felt)

grass cuttings with a little water

delivery tube   water

Warning!
Methane burns easily. A mixture of methane and air can explode.

Things to think about
* When rotting starts, will methane be produced straight away? Or will it be produced later on, when the microbes have used up all the oxygen in the generator?

What to do
- Assemble your generator and leave it. There should be enough microbes in the biodegradable material for digestion to start and gas to be produced. The microbes work best at a temperature of 35 °C.
- When you have collected enough gas, you may be able to test it to see if it burns. *Your teacher will show you how to do this safely.*

Landfill gas

Landfills (rubbish tips) are areas where both oxygen-loving and oxygen-hating microbes thrive. Methane gas is produced deep in the tip and carbon dioxide near the surface. The biogas from British landfill sites will soon be providing enough energy to save about half a million tonnes of coal every year.

6 Why is methane gas only produced deep in a tip?
7 Describe ways in which biogas might be used instead of coal.

The nodules on the roots of this bean plant contain microbes which take in nitrogen and make nitrates.

Nitrogen recycled

Living things need nitrogen for healthy growth. There is plenty in the air but plants and animals cannot use it directly. This is where microbes help. Microbes in the soil and in some roots use nitrogen in the air to make chemicals called **nitrates**. These are absorbed by the roots of plants. Microbes also make nitrates by feeding on animal droppings or the remains of dead animals and plants. Some microbes in wet soil work the other way. They release nitrogen gas from the nitrates which are around them in the soil.

8 How can nitrogen from the air end up in the body of an animal?
9 How can nitrogen in a dead plant or animal get back into the air again?

Even without a heater, it can be hot in a greenhouse. Sunlight passes through the glass and warms the things inside. The plants and soil radiate their warmth as invisible infrared radiation. Unlike sunlight, infrared cannot easily pass through glass. So some of its energy is trapped and the temperature in the greenhouse rises.

The greenhouse effect

Some of the gases in the atmosphere behave like the glass in a greenhouse. They trap the Sun's heat and keep the surface of the Earth warm. This is called the **greenhouse effect**. Without it, the Earth would be a much colder place. But over the past two centuries, amounts of these **greenhouse gases** have been rising. And the Earth has slowly started to warm up.

How heat is trapped in a greenhouse

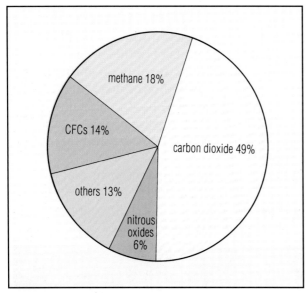

Greenhouse gases in the atmosphere

Look at the chart above.
1 What is the main greenhouse gas?
2 Where do you think the extra amounts of this gas might be coming from?
3 Where could the methane be coming from?
4 Why is the problem with the greenhouse effect recent compared with the age of the Earth?

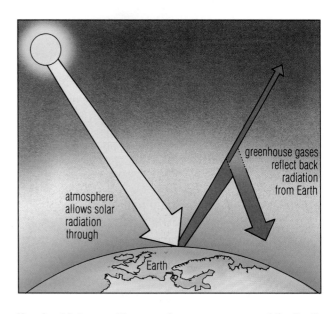

How heat is trapped by greenhouse gases around the Earth

Rainforest covers 7% of the Earth's land surface. But an area the size of Belgium is being burnt down every year as more and more land is used for industry and agriculture.
5 Can you think of *two* reasons why the greenhouse effect would be reduced if the burning of rainforests was stopped? What are they?

Problems of a warmer world

Scientists think they know what will happen if the greenhouse effect warms up the Earth. Parts of the polar ice caps will melt, making sea levels rise. Temperature changes will alter the climate. Some places may be hotter and drier. Others may be wetter.

6 What would be the effect on plants, animals and people in this country:
a if it became hotter and drier?
b if sea levels rose?

One possible result of the greenhouse effect.

The ozone layer

The ozone layer is a region of gases high in the Earth's atmosphere. It contains the highest concentration of **ozone**, a special type of oxygen which screens us from some of the Sun's ultraviolet rays. Ultraviolet can give you a sun tan, but it also causes skin cancer.

Chemical processes in the atmosphere are always making and destroying ozone. But some of the gases we produce on Earth are getting into the atmosphere and destroying too much ozone. People have been especially worried about gases called CFCs (Chlorofluorocarbons). CFCs have been used in aerosols, refrigerators and freezers and in making plastic foam packaging. Many manufacturers are now replacing CFCs with gases which are more 'ozone friendly'.

7 Why do we need the protection of the ozone layer?
8 What do you think 'ozone friendly' means?
9 Why is the use of CFCs being cut back?
10 What would be the other advantage of cutting the use of CFCs? (You may find a clue on the opposite page.)
11 Instead of CFCs, some companies are starting to use gases similar to methane. What problems would this cause?

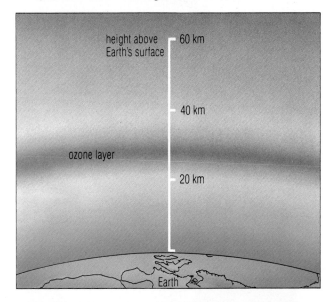

In the past, many people have felt that, if you bought food from a fast-food takeaway, you were helping to destroy the ozone layer.

12 Why might people think this?
13 Some fast-food companies are trying to be more 'ozone friendly'. What action could they be taking?

113

High Street, Oxford, in 1900

High Street, Oxford, today

Then and now

The photographs on the opposite page both show the same place. But one was taken about 90 years after the other.

1. Study the photographs carefully. Make a note of all the changes which have taken place during the time between them.
2. With your group, discuss the scientific and technological advances which have made these changes possible. Make a list of your ideas.
3. What environmental problems might the people in the older photograph have had to cope with?
4. What extra environmental problems have our modern lifestyles brought us? Use examples from the two photographs to support your ideas.

Predicting the future

When the first photograph was taken, most of the traffic was horse-drawn vehicles. These brought their own pollution problems. There were deposits of horse droppings in the street! As traffic got worse and worse, someone predicted that, within a hundred years, the streets of London would be 20 centimetres deep in horse droppings!

5. Why was that prediction wrong?

Imagine that, as scientists, your group has been given the job of predicting what the pollution from city traffic will be like in 100 years time.

6. What things will you need to know before you can start making your prediction?
7. What new inventions or changes in peoples' lifestyles might affect the actual amount of pollution produced?
8. When you have finished your discussions make a presentation of your ideas.

Closer to home

Now compare the changes which have taken place in an area close to your home.

9. See if you can find pictures, photographs or postcards showing old scenes from the area where you live now.
10. Make a presentation which illustrates the scientific and technological changes which have happened in your area during this century.
11. Describe the changes to your local environment which have happened during the same time.
12. Are there any links between your answers to the last two questions? If so describe them. Say whether you think the changes have been for better or worse.

Air is not always as clean as it should be. There can be all sorts of unpleasant and harmful substances mixed in with it. For example: smoke, and gases such as sulphur dioxide. These are called **pollutants**. They cause **air pollution**.

1 What things cause air pollution? Make a list of your ideas.

Smog is a mixture of fog, smoke and chemical pollutants. At one time, many industrial towns in Britain suffered from it. Here is a short article for you to read about smog:

Smog over Los Angeles, USA

In December 1952, London was smothered in smog for five days. It was so thick and dirty that white collars became almost black in half an hour. Four thousand people died as a result of the smog. The victims were mainly elderly people and those with chest illnesses.

After the Great Smog of 1952, much research was carried out to try to find the sources of the pollution. As a result, in 1956, the first Clear Air Act was passed in Britain in an attempt to clean up the atmosphere.

Stricter regulations were set for the emissions of smoke and chemicals like sulphur dioxide from chimneys of factories and power stations. Some areas were declared 'smokeless' zones and houses in these areas could only burn smokeless fuels.

The graphs on the right show some of the measurements made after the introduction of the Clean Air Act.

2 Describe in words what changes the graphs are showing.

3 What did the researchers decide were the most likely causes of smog?

4 From the information you have seen, decide whether you think that the Clean Air Act was successful.

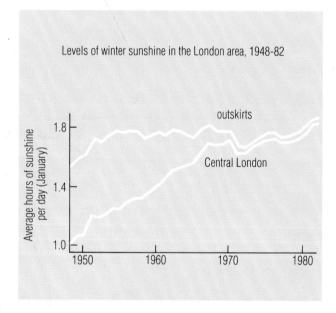

Levels of winter sunshine in the London area, 1948-82

outskirts

Central London

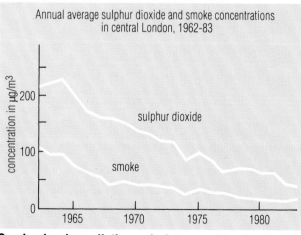

Annual average sulphur dioxide and smoke concentrations in central London, 1962-83

sulphur dioxide

smoke

Graphs showing pollution and winter sunshine data for the London area

Air pollution survey

Lichens are tiny, simple plants which spread over tree trunks, rocks, roofs and walls. They are a good guide to air pollution because some types are more easily poisoned by sulphur dioxide than others. **Shrubby lichens** (the ones that stick out most) are the most sensitive. **Leafy lichens** are less sensitive. **Crusty lichens** are the least sensitive of all. As a rule, the more a lichen sticks out, the cleaner the air.

You can see some lichens on the right. Also shown is another simple plant called *pleurococcus*. This looks like a green powder. It can stand much more sulphur dioxide than the lichens.

5 Look at the photographs. Why might you see the plants in this order if you travelled from the centre of a city to the outskirts?

Investigate

■ Carry out a survey of sulphur dioxide pollution by studying lichens and *pleurococcus* in your area.
■ Make a map or leaflet to show your findings.

Local pollution

The smoke from cigarettes causes pollution in small spaces like rooms.

6 If you are near someone who is smoking, you are a 'passive smoker'. What does this mean?

Jobs like sawing and quarrying make large amounts of dust. Face masks are recommended for jobs like this.

7 Make a list of DIY jobs which produce airborne pollutants.
8 Which of these pollutants could be filtered out by a mask?
9 Find out as much as you can about 'industrial diseases' caused by workers inhaling airborne pollutants.

Pleurococcus

Crusty lichen

Leafy lichen

Shrubby lichen

Outskirts of city

H3.2 Acid rain

Rain is naturally slightly acid. It slowly attacks stone, paint and metalwork on buildings. Over the past two hundred years, the problem has got worse. This is because pollutants in the air have been dissolving in rain and making the acid stronger. Acid rain can damage trees and other plants. It can reach streams, rivers and lakes where it can poison fish and other forms of life.

1 How can acid rain get into a tree?
2 How can acid rain become concentrated in a lake?

Scientists use the **pH scale** to measure how strongly acid different things are. To find the pH number of a liquid, you dip **universal indicator paper** into it. Then you compare the colour of the paper with colours on a chart. This tells you the pH number. You can see part of the pH scale with typical colours on the right.

3 What is the pH number of unpolluted rainwater?
4 What is the pH number of the most heavily polluted rain?
5 Measure the pH number of a sample of rain in your area.

strong acid		
	pH 1	battery acid
increasing acidity	pH 2	lemon juice vinegar
	pH 3	orange juice
	pH 4	
	pH 5	pure rain
	pH 6	
neutral	pH 7	distilled water

acid rain

colour of indicator paper

Damage survey

In areas of high air pollution, the damage to stonework is much worse than elsewhere. Stones like sandstone, limestone and marble are especially at risk.

Investigate

- In your area, see if you can find some natural materials which have been exposed to air pollution. These could be old buildings, statues, or gravestones.
- Compare parts which have been exposed to different amounts of pollution. Record their position. For example are they inside or outside, facing the wind or away from it?
- Prepare a report on your observations.

The effect of acid rain

Tree damage

If a tree starts to die, it is not easy to tell whether acid rain is the cause. The photographs show trees which may have been damaged by acid rain.

6 Describe the appearance of the trees.
7 Describe how you would expect normal trees to look after a long, warm, dry summer. How does this compare with the signs of damage by acid rain?
8 Explain why it is difficult for scientists to estimate the true scale of acid rain pollution.

Looking for causes

Scientists now think they know what causes acid rain. Power stations and factories which burn coal and oil give out sulphur dioxide. Car exhausts give out nitrogen oxides and some sulphur dioxide as well. These chemicals dissolve in rainclouds to form sulphuric and nitric acids which fall as acid rain.

The map shows areas in Europe where damage to forests, lakes and streams has been recorded. It also shows the main European producers of sulphur dioxide pollution. With your group:

9 Find the following countries or regions on the map: *Britain, France, Germany, Poland, Scandinavia, Spain, Switzerland, Romania, Yugoslavia.*
10 List the countries which produce the greatest amounts of sulphur dioxide.
11 List the countries most affected by acid rain.
12 How do you think pollutants from one country could affect the rain in another?
13 Explain whether you think that industrial pollution could be responsible for the damage to forests, lakes and streams.
14 What type of damage from acid rain is not shown on the map?

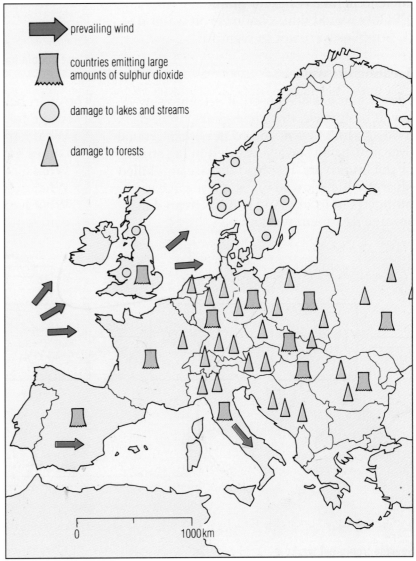

→ prevailing wind

countries emitting large amounts of sulphur dioxide

◯ damage to lakes and streams

△ damage to forests

0   1000 km

In Britain, each person uses about 140 litres of water per day.

1. Make a list of all the ways in which you use water.
2. For each item on your list, estimate the volume (in litres) of the water you use.
3. Estimate how much water is used for family chores such as washing clothes, dishes and a car.
4. Compare your estimate with the average figure.

In this country there is usually plenty of water for our homes. The cost is fairly low. So we tend to take water for granted.

5. How would you economise on water if supplies were not so plentiful.

Some people have to collect their water

Treating the waste

Once water has been used, it becomes sewage. It has grease, dirt, detergents, unused food and toilet waste mixed in with it. At one time, untreated sewage was left in the streets or put into rivers. It spread disease and killed off water life. Nowadays, some sewage is pumped out to sea. And some is treated in **sewage treatment works**

The chart below shows you what happens in a sewage treatment works.

6. What happens to the purified water which comes out of the treatment works?
7. What gases are produced by the works?
8. What do you think makes these gases?
9. What happens to the other waste which comes out of the works?

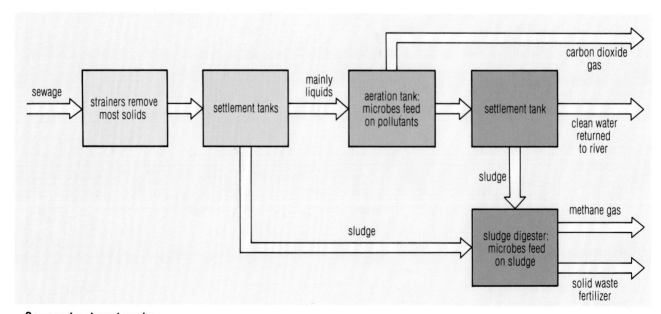

Sewage treatment works

1858 was the year of the 'Great Stink'. The smell from the sewage polluting the River Thames was so strong that politicians fled from the Houses of Parliament.

River pollution

Factories which need large amounts of water are usually built close to rivers. They take water from the river and discharge their waste water further downstream. By law, they must treat their waste water before discharging it. But industrial accidents can happen for example in 1986, there was a fire at a chemical factory near the River Rhine in Germany. The water used to fight the fire washed 900 tonnes of pesticides and mercury into the river. Half a million fish and eels died as a result.

10 Why can rivers become polluted even though there are laws to prevent it? How many reasons can you think of?

Pollutants on the farm

Materials from farms can be highly polluting. For example, animal slurry ('muck') is 100 times more polluting than untreated sewage from a house. Agricultural pollutants can end up in rivers or even in the water supply. Look at the table on the right. It shows the number of convictions for pollution offences from 1980 to 1986.

11 What caused most pollution problems?
12 Which offences appear to be on the increase?
13 Which types of pollution would be made worse by a long spell of wet weather?
14 Why must farms be careful not to cause pollution?

In fish farms, huge numbers of fish are kept in 'pens'(enclosures) in rivers or lochs. Chemicals are added to the water to keep down disease. When the fish are fed, any uneaten food sinks to the bottom and is washed away with the fish excrement.

15 Someone says 'Fish farms can't cause pollution because it is natural for fish to live in rivers and lochs'. What reply would you give?

River polluted by sewage

Convictions for pollution offences				
Source of pollution	1980	1982	1984	1986
Slurry stores	12	22	42	48
Silage effluent	8	15	32	52
Land run off	9	3	3	12
Yard water	3	14	9	5
Sheep dip	0	0	0	0
Pesticides	0	1	0	1
Vegetable washings	0	2	0	4
Oil spillages	0	1	2	2

Fish in a fish farm

121

H3.4 A watch on pollution

A team of scientists spent several months studying snowfalls on the Cairngorm Mountains in Scotland. They found that the colour of each fresh snowfall could change from day to day. Some snow was pinkish. Some had black, sooty particles in it. The pH number of the snow also varied a lot.

The snow on the Cairngorms started as water droplets in clouds. By the time the snow landed on the mountainside, it contained pollutants.

1 How do you think the snow could have become polluted?

2 Why might the pH number and the colour vary from day to day?

The Cairngorm area has a small local population and the main industry is tourism. The scientists thought that most of the pollutants in the snow probably came from places a long way away.

3 Would you agree with the scientists? Explain your answer.

4 What observations and measurements would the scientists need to make so that they could find out where the pollutants were coming from.

Present problems

Our modern lifestyle has created many new pollution problems. Answer these with your group:

5 Choose one example of a pollution problem which we face today.

6 Discuss the different ways in which people are adding to the problem.

7 Decide how the following people could help solve the problem:
- scientists
- industrialists
- politicians
- ordinary citizens

8 Find an interesting way of presenting your conclusions. For example, you could write a short play.

The Cairngorms

We can only make recommendations. It's up to individuals to decide whether they will follow our advice.

The pollution we see today is due to the negligence of the previous government.

We live in a consumer society. As soon as a new product is put on the market, the old hi-fi's condemned to the scrap heap.

Acid rain survey

Investigate

Measure the pH number of some rain samples from your area. Look for any changes and what might be causing them.

You need
Container for collecting rain, universal indicator paper.

What to do
- Collect and test your rain samples.
- Draw a graph or chart to show your results.
- See if you can find out about any possible sources of air pollution in your area.
- Look for patterns in your results. For example, is there a link between the pH number and the wind direction? Can you tell where the pollution is coming from?
- Prepare a report on your findings.

Useful information
- You may need to keep records for weeks or even months.
- It might be a good idea to record the wind direction and strength as well as the pH number of the rain.
- Even unpolluted rain is slightly acid.

Date rain fell	pH of rainwater collected	wind strength and direction (from daily paper)
1st June	6	light wind from West
2nd June	4	light wind from West
6th June	5	light southerly wind
9th June	3	strong northerly wind

Past problems

Here are some of the ways in which scientists have helped solve pollution problems in the past:
- by finding out about the causes of pollution.
- by suggesting ways in which pollution could be reduced.
- by helping engineers and technologists to design new products with fewer pollutants in them.

9 Choose one example of pollution which was common in the past and is now less of a problem.

10 Describe the causes of this pollution.

11 Explain how the pollution affected the lives of the people at that time.

12 Explain how scientists have helped to reduce the problem.

Daily Post

New exhaust systems mean cleaner air

Emissions from car exhausts in the 90s will be cleaner, thanks to new lean burn engines and catalytic converters fitted to exhaust systems

Air fares rise

Stepping stones

Meanings

Someone asks you to explain what the word 'environment' means.

1 What would you say?

The word 'environment' can have slightly different meanings depending on how it is used. The extracts below all appeared in a science magazine. Each uses the word 'environment' but in a slightly different way.

2 Read the extracts carefully.

3 Write down the meaning of the word 'environment' as it is used in each article or advertisement.

4 How do these meanings compare with your own ideas on the word 'environment'?

5 Write a short description of your area using the word 'environment.'

All electric

I live in a flat which is all electric. I don't have any gas appliances or coal fires, so I am not using up any fossil fuels.

6 Think of four different ways in which Les might be using equipment or services which depend on fossil fuels.

7 How would you explain to Les that his claim was incorrect?

Norwegian scientist awarded medal for her 'outstanding contribution to scientific discovery in the Antarctic'

At 38, Monica Kristensen is already a veteran of 15 scientific missions to the Arctic and the Antarctic. Ms Kristensen admits that she has chosen a tough way of life. In a recent interview she explained: 'The environment in Antarctica is very hostile, so it is important to be part of a team of people with the right skills, mentality and attitude.'

A career in Environmental Microbiology

We are looking for a dedicated microbiologist to join our research team. The successful candidate will be involved in carrying out a range of studies to ensure the environmental safety of our company's products.

EEC Environment Ministers meet in Brussels

Agreement has finally been reached to limit the pollution emitted by small cars. By the end of 1992, all new cars with engines smaller than 1.4 litres will be required to meet strict limits. This will involve the use of catalytic converters.

Environment friendly
Printed on recycled paper

Factory waste

A factory discharges its waste water into a nearby river. A check on the river quality in January showed that it was satisfactory. Six months later, another check shows that the river is moderately polluted downstream from the factory. The management says that nothing has changed in the factory. They are producing exactly the same goods as they were before.

8 What else could have caused the increase in river pollution?

9 How could pollution be avoided in future?

Biogas

Biogas can be used as a fuel.

10 What is biogas?

11 What things can be used as a source of biogas?

12 What are the advantages of using biogas as a fuel?

13 What are the disadvantages?

Acid rain

Scientists agree that acid rain exists. But they don't all agree on what things are causing the pollution.

14 Describe the evidence available.

15 Give your ideas about where the worst pollution might be coming from.

Keep or return?

In the early 1800s, Lord Elgin removed some sculptures from the Parthenon in Athens. He gave them to the British Museum. Now called the Elgin marbles, they have been well preserved in the clean air of the museum. Other stonework on buildings in Athens has been badly affected by air pollution.

16 Some people think that the Elgin marbles should be returned to their proper place. Others think that they need protecting from air pollution. What do you think?

The Parthenon, Athens

Elgin marble

Index

Acknowledgements

Allsport: pp 78 (top left, top right), 80 (top right); Heather Angel: pp 54 (centre), 55 (bottom left); 74 (all), 108 (left), 113 (top right), 116 (top), 117, 119 (top right), 121 (top right); Barnaby's Picture Library: pp 22 (right), 26 (bottom); BBC: p 110 (bottom right); J Allan Cash: pp 17 (top right), 38 (top right, centre right), 41 (bottom right), 49 (top left), 50 (top left), 52 (top right, bottom), 60 (top right), 62 (centre right), 82, 98 (bottom right), 99, 100 (bottom right), 104 (right), 105 (left & bottom right); Bruce Coleman: pp 26, 45 (all), 47 (top left, top right), 49 (top right), 50 (top right, bottom right), 52 (centre), 68 (top left & right), 73 (bottom right), 79 (bottom left), 85 (right), 90 (bottom right), 93 (left), 98 (top right), 99, 101 (top right), 102 (top right), 117 (bottom right), 125 (right); Crown Copyright: p 43; Dundee Meterological Office: p 38; Evans Mary Evans Picture Library: p 29; GeoScience Features: pp 51 (centre), 59 (top right), 62 (top); Griggs Susan Griggs Agency: p 17 (top left); Robert Harding: pp 108 (centre), p 122 (right); Philip Harris Ltd: p 40; Holt Studios: p 111 (bottom right); Hulton Deutsch Collection: p 79 (bottom right); I M Keill: p 46 (top right); Long Ashton Research Centre: p 91 (top right); Patricia Moffett: pp 110, 118; Oxford County Council: p 114 (top); Planet Earth: p 10 (top right); Press Association: p 100 (top right); Science Photo Library: pp 73 (right), 80 (centre), 83 (bottom), Sharp Ltd: p 23; Ronald Sheridan: pp 45 (top), 125 (bottom right) Spectrum: p 120; Telegraph Colour Library: pp 71 (top right), 77; Tropix Photo Library: p 93 (left); A C Waltham pp 46 (bottom right), 47 (centre), 48 (top right), 51, 54 (top right, bottom right), 58 (top), 59 (left, centre), 62 (top right), 63 (top right); C James Webb: p 22 (left). Zefa Photographic Library: pp 46 (centre right), 48 (top left), 84 (top right), 102 (centre), 108 (right).

Additional photography by Chris Honeywell and Michelle Tither

The illustrations are by: Ed Carr, Nick Duffy, Nick Hawken, Jim McCarthy, Mark Oliver, Lynne Riding, Mike Sharp, Tony Simpson, Julie Tolliday, David Watson Emma Whiting and Chris Duggan.

Oxford University Press
Walton Street
Oxford OX2 6DP

Oxford New York
Athens Auckland Bangkok Bombay
Calcutta Cape Town Dar es Salaam Delhi
Florence Hong Kong Istanbul Karachi
Kuala Lumpur Madras Madrid Melbourne
Mexico City Nairobi Paris Singapore
Taipei Tokyo Toronto
and associated companies in
Berlin Ibadan

© Stephen Pople, Paul Denley et al 1991

First published 1991
Reprinted 1992, 1994

ISBN 019 914330 7

Printed in Hong Kong